Meet the Pit B

- Historians have traced the Pit Bull back to ancient Greece.

- The Pit Bull, also called the American Pit Bull Terrier, is considered the strongest dog in the world for its size.

- A Pit Bull was the most decorated hero dog during World War I.

- The first "Bull-and-Terriers" imported to America were for the purpose of blood sports.

- The Pit Bull is described as being reliable, hard-working, people-loving, and multi-talented.

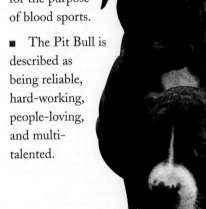

- The _____ and pleasant nature, make him an ideal candidate for therapy work with people.

- Pit Bulls have a strong desire to please their owners.

- Pit Bulls have expressive faces and some can actually smile! When greeting their owners and special friends, the dogs may give a large toothy grin, raising their upper lip until their muzzle wrinkles and their eyes narrow.

- Pit Bulls require minimal grooming. In fact, all they need is five minutes a day.

- The most famous Pit Bull was "Pete" from the *Little Rascals*.

Consulting Editor

IAN DUNBAR PH.D., MRCVS

Featuring Photographs by

WINTER CHURCHILL PHOTOGRAPHY

Howell Book House

An Imprint of Macmillan General Reference USA
A Pearson Education Macmillan Company
1633 Broadway
New York, NY 10019

Macmillan Publishing books may be purchased for business or sales promotional use. For information please write: Special Markets Department, Macmillan Publishing USA, 1633 Broadway, New York, NY 10019.

Library of Congress Cataloging-in-Publication Data

The essential pit bull.
p. cm.
Includes bibliographical references and index.
ISBN 1-58245-022-6
1. Pit bull. I. Howell Book House.
SF429.A72E87 1999 98-46323
636.755'9—dc21 CIP

Manufactured in the United States of America
10 9 8 7 6 5 4 3 2

Series Director: Michele Matrisciani
Production Team: Carrie Allen, Heather Pope, and Christina Van Camp
Book Design: Paul Costello
Photography: Courtesy of Diana Robinson: 77
All other photos by Winter Churchill Photography.

ARE YOU READY?!

☐ Have you prepared your home and your family for your new pet?

☐ Have you gotten the proper supplies you'll need to care for your dog?

☐ Have you found a veterinarian that you (and your dog) are comfortable with?

☐ Have you thought about how you want your dog to behave?

☐ Have you arranged your schedule to accommodate your dog's needs for exercise and attention?

No matter what stage you're at with your dog—still thinking about getting one, or he's already part of the family—this Essential guide will provide you with the practical information you need to understand and care for your canine companion. Of course you're ready—you have this book!

Pit Bull

SIGHT

Pit Bulls can detect movement at a greater distance than we can, but they can't see as well up close. They can also see better in less light, but can't distinguish many colors.

SOUND

Pit Bulls, like all dogs, can hear about four times better than we can, and they can hear high-pitched sounds especially well.

TASTE

Pit Bulls have fewer taste buds than we do, so they're more likely to try anything—and usually do, which is why it's important for their owners to monitor their food intake. Dogs are omnivorous, which means they eat meat as well as vegetables.

TOUCH

Pit Bulls are social animals and love to be petted, groomed and played with.

SMELL

A Pit Bull's nose is his greatest sensory organ. A dog's sense of smell is so great he can follow a trail that's weeks old, detect odors diluted to one-millionth the concentration we'd need to notice them, even sniff out a person underwater!

Getting to Know Your Pit Bull

Robust, quick and brimming with vigor, today's Pit Bull is an intelligent roughneck who wants to please and is ever hopeful of being a lap dog. Supremely confident, he views the world as a giant playhouse created especially for his amusement and is something of a perennial puppy: He enjoys playing tug, catch and other games, well into old age. Good-natured with children, the Pit Bull has the sturdiness not to mind if his tail or toe is accidentally stepped on, and possesses the capacity to play for hours. The Pit Bull also enjoys training sessions, and learns quickly as long as his trainer is fair, firm and praises a job well done.

THE PERSONALITY OF A PIT BULL

Contrary to popular hysteria and media hype, the dogfighting

The Pit Bull is consistently friendly and easy to train.

fraternity neither bred nor trained the Pit Bull to be aggressive toward people. Imagine anyone wanting to work with a dangerous dog for hours every day in a keep! Because they were handled in all sorts of circumstances, fighting dogs had to be friendly, steady and reliable around people.

Today, a properly bred Pit Bull is so exuberantly happy upon meeting her owner's friends (or even friendly strangers) that new owners sometimes worry that their dog is too sweet and fun-loving to protect their home and family.

The protective instinct of the Pit Bull usually surfaces when the dog is around 10 months old,

although this time can vary by three months or so. A Pit Bull with the correct temperament will not threaten to attack a human without a very good reason, but will begin becoming alert to the doorbell or the sight of a stranger approaching the house. The young dog doesn't need any encouragement to guard his owners and his home, and is best allowed to use his own discretion. There have been numerous cases proving the exceptional ability of the family Pit Bull to sense, and signal to his family, when a person or a situation could be dangerous. Exceptions to letting a Pit Bull guard at will should be made if the dog is overly aggressive, or if he is destined to be used in a specific type of protection work.

Pit Bulls enjoy being the center of attention, are confident enough to adapt to unusual surroundings and have a higher than usual tolerance for pain. These traits place them among the top breeds in canine therapy work. They gleefully show off their obedience training or their favorite tricks at children's hospitals, senior centers and schools for the mentally and physically challenged.

Pit Bulls exude self-confidence, not only at home, but in the park or noisy city street as well. While the degree of aggression toward other dogs varies between individuals, Pit Bulls are often so self-assured that they ignore dogs of other breeds rather than pick fights to prove themselves. But this is not always the case. You should be aware that from 6 months of age on, your Pit Bull could suddenly develop a desire to test his strength against other dogs. That's one of the reasons why training (see chapter 8) is so important.

3

Pit Bulls love to be around people.

Pit Bulls love to show off and be the center of attention.

COMICAL COMMUNICATION

One reason Pit Bulls are so much fun is that their faces are so expressive. Some of them actually smile. These special canine clowns greet their owners, and sometimes other human friends, with a large toothy grin. They make this amusing mug by raising their upper lip until their muzzle wrinkles and their eyes narrow. When smiling, many Pit Bulls also tap their front feet up and down in a happy dance, demonstrating their delight at the sight of a loved one. While this facial expression is comical and endearing to those who know the breed, it has been known to terrify friendly strangers.

DEFECTIVE DOGS?

A perfectly nice puppy might grow up to be unfriendly because his owner encourages him to become mean. Unfair and overly harsh discipline can reduce an outgoing pup to a cowering bundle of nerves—the first step on the way to biting out of fear. Patience, persistence and praise are essential when working with puppies, and no one should ever train a dog of any age when they are in a bad mood. Neglect probably negates more happy-go-lucky puppy personalities than any other sin of dog ownership. Seldom done on purpose, it just seems to happen when the novelty of having a puppy wears off. Soon the youngster is constantly confined to a crate, tie-out chain, kennel or yard, with no human contact except at feeding time. Lonely, bored and isolated from his human family, the puppy will be unable to develop his unique character, and could become aloof, shy or cranky.

PERSONALITY TRAITS OF HAPPY PIT BULL OWNERS

If dogs could choose their owners instead of the other way around, Pit

CHARACTERISTICS OF THE PIT BULL

Strong resolve to please his owner

Protective instinct—makes him a natural guardian

Enjoys being the center of attention

Highly trainable

Robust and energetic

Bulls would probably look for owners who are blessed with high spirits and the joy of living. The Pit Bull still wants to frolic long after her muzzle turns gray, and most contented owners enjoy playing with their dogs. In fact, many people

5

The Pit Bull's sense of humor is not lost on other four-legged family members.

Successful Pit Bull owners are high-spirited and know how to handle their dogs.

consider the breed's perennial puppiness an endearing plus!

Many Pit Bull owners are enthusiastic, competitive or both. Since the breed shares its owners' enthusiasm and excels in the showring, obedience competition, weight pulling, agility demonstrations and Schutzhund, many exciting sports are available. Owners who have enthusiasm but don't want to become involved in weekend competitions may find volunteer work with a pet therapy group very fulfilling.

Good owners of Pit Bulls are able to handle their dogs. What's important is that the Pit Bull must be trained: Successful owners know this and are willing to take on the responsibility and joy of training their dog. If the dog will be handled by a child, the child should understand the basics of training.

ATTRACTIVE OPPOSITES

Strong and sensitive; rowdy, yet gentle; outgoing, but devoted; easily fired up, but highly trainable; mischievous, yet sensible; energetic and serene; peaceful, but ever alert— these apparent contradictions could all describe the Pit Bull. A zest for life, combined with occasional attempts to outwit his owner, endears the breed to many, but could be considered an inconvenience by others. Some people would enjoy a little less dog.

Spending lots of time with your puppy will help him become a happy, well-adjusted dog.

7

CHAPTER TWO

Homecoming

A little advance planning will help you enjoy your new dog and will keep her happy and healthy. Before bringing your puppy home, you will want to have nutritious puppy food in the cupboard and the address and phone number of a trusted veterinarian.

EXERCISE—Leading an active life will make your Pit Bull live longer, look healthier and behave better. Brisk walks are good for both of you. If you don't want to walk every day, teach your dog to play ball or Frisbee and you can exercise her while sitting or standing, or give her a securely fenced play area with a couple of dog toys and an old car tire, and she will exercise herself.

SLEEPY TIME—Young puppies tire easily and should be allowed to sleep until they wake up on their own. Even the healthiest, happiest pups become limp as dishrags when it's snooze time, and when puppies are young, naps are sudden, frequent and often short. As puppies grow older, they sleep less often but stay asleep for a longer time.

PUPPY-PROOFING YOUR HOME

Until your puppy is housebroken and has stopped teething, confine her to one easily cleaned room of your home when no one is home to supervise her. The kitchen or bathroom is ideal. A wire mesh baby gate often works better than a door when confining a young puppy to a room.

TAKE PRECAUTIONS

To make the room (and the rest of your home) safe when your Pit Bull is unsupervised, put all cleaning

HOUSEHOLD DANGERS

Curious puppies and inquisitive dogs get into trouble not because they are bad, but simply because they want to investigate the world around them. It's our job to protect our dogs from harmful substances, like the following:

In the Garage

antifreeze

garden supplies, like snail and slug bait, pesticides, fertilizers, mouse and rat poisons

In the House

cleaners, especially pine oil

perfumes, colognes, aftershaves

medications, vitamins

office and craft supplies

electric cords

chicken or turkey bones

chocolate, onions

some house and garden plants, like ivy, oleander and poinsettia

9

Puppy-proofing your home will help prevent your puppy from ingesting anything harmful.

identify them and look them up to make sure they are not poisonous (many common houseplants are). All plants should be placed out of your dog's reach; extra precautions are necessary with poisonous plants.

Expect an unsupervised puppy to teethe on whatever is reachable. It's important to close cupboard doors because puppies have been known to chomp on anything from raw potatoes to fountain pens and Brillo pads.

THE GREAT CRATE

Buy your puppy a crate that is large enough for a grown Pit Bull to stand up and turn around in comfortably. The crate will be a tremendous help with housebreaking because your dog will soon learn not to soil her bed. It can also serve as a safe playpen, so she can't damage

10

Puppies thrive on a set routine that includes exercise, eating, rest and play.

agents, antifreeze, pesticides, drugs and other household, garage or garden chemicals out of her reach. If it isn't possible to eliminate electrical wires that your dog can reach, coat them with Bitter Apple, a safe, bad-tasting substance created to prevent chewing. If you have houseplants,

Expect an unsupervised puppy to teethe on anything available.

A crate will give your Pit Bull a safe place to rest or play.

furniture or swallow something dangerous when you are away or asleep. The crate should be placed in your dog's puppy-proofed room, right up front near the baby gate.

Your Pit Bull's crate should be snug, soft and comfortable inside. The bedding should be easy to change and not dangerous if chewed or swallowed. Every time you put your dog in her crate, toss a favorite toy or a special treat in the crate ahead of her. Say "crate" and, as gently as possible, put her in and shut the door. She may cry the first few times she is introduced to her crate, but if you walk away and don't take her out of the crate until she settles down, she'll soon become accustomed to it.

BASIC SUPPLIES

SAFE TOYS—Toys are not an extra but a necessity. Your Pit Bull needs something safe on which to gnaw

PUPPY ESSENTIALS

To prepare yourself and your family for your puppy's homecoming, and to be sure your pup has what she needs, you should obtain the following:

Food and Water Bowls: One for each. We recommend stainless steel or heavy crockery—something solid but easy to clean.

Bed and/or Crate Pad: Something soft, washable and big enough for your soon-to-be-adult dog.

Crate: Make housetraining easier and provide a safe, secure den for your dog with a crate—it only looks like a cage to you!

Toys: As much fun to buy as they are for your pup to play with. Don't overwhelm your puppy with too many toys, though, especially the first few days she's home. And be sure to include something hollow you can stuff with goodies, like a Kong.

I.D. Tag: Inscribed with your name and phone number.

Collar: An adjustable buckle collar is best. Remember, your pup's going to grow fast!

Leash: Style is nice, but durability and your comfort while holding it count, too. You can't go wrong with leather for most dogs.

Grooming Supplies: The proper brushes, special shampoo, toenail clippers, a toothbrush and doggy toothpaste.

while she is teething, and should have toys available all the time.

Rawhide chew toys are a traditional favorite, but there have been rare accidents when a torn chunk from a rawhide toy got caught in a dog's throat and choked her. So give your dog rawhide only when you are home and in the same room with her, and don't choose rawhide for her crate toy.

Squeaky toys (of lightweight rubber or plastic) are popular with pups, but they are only safe when you are either watching or joining in the play. These toys are easily torn apart by Pit Bull puppies and swallowed, dangerous squeaker mechanism and all. Keep your dog's squeaky toy out of her reach and bring it out every few days for some special minutes of fun.

Chew toys made of hard nylon are safe in your Pit Bull's mouth even when you aren't home. Puppies prefer the softer, equally safe, gummy-type nylon chews. Solid, hard rubber toys are also safe and fun, but eventually your dog may be able to mangle even those labeled "indestructible." When you see that she is gouging pieces out of her rubber toys, do not leave her alone with them.

Don't forget to supply your Pit Bull with some chew toys to keep her occupied.

Your Pit Bull needs food and water bowls that are easy to clean and difficult to tip over.

Providing your Pit Bull with a completely fenced-in yard is the best way to ensure that he will not be lost or stolen.

Braided rope toys are fun for games of tug, and good for helping to keep your dog's teeth tartar free. If she starts unraveling her rope, don't leave her alone with it, as swallowing the string could cause intestinal problems. For the ultimate puppy treat, buy a sterilized bone toy and stuff it with cheese. This crate toy will keep your dog occupied for a long time.

PRACTICAL DOG DISHES—These are easy to clean and difficult to tip over, and your Pit Bull should have one for food and another for water.

The food dish should be washed after each use, and the water dish should be refilled with fresh water frequently and washed thoroughly once a day. When selecting dishes, remember that as your dog grows, so will the size of her meals.

GROOMING GIZMOS—Unlike hairy breeds, Pit Bulls have easy-to-care-for coats. All you need to keep your dog beautiful is a brush with short, soft to medium bristles, heavy-duty toenail clippers, a good quality pH-balanced dog shampoo and a soft toothbrush.

FIRST COLLAR AND LEASH—

Wait until you bring your Pit Bull home to buy a collar, so you can get a perfect fit. The collar should apply no pressure to her neck, but it shouldn't be loose enough to slip over her head. It should be flat, made of nylon webbing or leather, with a buckle and ring for attaching the leash. Check the fit of your dog's collar weekly. Puppies grow fast, and collars must be replaced immediately when they become too small.

The leash should be 5 to 6 feet long and made of leather, nylon webbing or some other strong, flexible fabric. Neither the collar nor the leash should be made of chain. You may want a chain training collar as a teaching aid when your Pit Bull is older, but she should wear it only for training, not as her regular collar.

IDENTIFY YOUR DOG

It is a terrible thing to think about, but your dog could somehow, someday, get lost or stolen. For safety's sake, every dog should wear a buckle collar with an identification tag. A tag is the first thing a stranger will look for on a lost dog. Inscribe the tag with your dog's name and your name and phone number.

There are two ways to permanently identify your dog. The first is a tattoo, placed on the inside of your dog's thigh. The tattoo should be your social security number or your dog's registration number. The second is a microchip, a rice-sized pellet that is inserted under the dog's skin at the base of the neck, between the shoulder blades. When a scanner is passed over the dog, it will beep, notifying the person that the dog has a chip. The scanner will then show a code, identifying the dog.

15

To Good Health

FIRST THINGS FIRST

Your Pit Bull may never encounter any of the following problems, however, it is important that you are aware of a few inherited disorders specific to the breed.

SARCOPTIC MANGE—Sarcoptic mange is caused by mites. It will make your Pit Bull itch, and you will see tiny red bumps and patchy, crusty areas on his body, legs or stomach. Take your dog to the veterinarian immediately. The condition is treatable and will respond to topical medication.

FOLLICULAR MANGE—This mange is caused by a different type of mite. Also called demodectic mange or red mange, this condition may or may not make your Pit Bull itch. Whether it bothers him or not, you will notice small, circular, moth-eaten–like patches, usually on his head and along his back, sides and neck. Juvenile cases, involving a young dog with only a few patches, might be stress-related. Some females, for example, get a patch or two of mange when they come into season for the first time. Your veterinarian has medication to clear up this condition, but if your Pit Bull ever gets a generalized case of this mange (covering much of his body), don't use him for breeding, as he could pass the problem on to his young.

FLEABITE ALLERGIC

DERMATITIS—This is an allergic reaction to fleabites. It can occur at any time in your dog's life, sometimes causing an allergic reaction in a dog who didn't previously react to fleabites. Symptoms include intense itching combined with reddened, swollen and hot skin. If your Pit Bull becomes allergic to fleabites, he will continuously scratch, lick and even bite at the affected area. Without treatment, the area will eventually become dry and scaly, the skin will thicken and the hair will fall out. Prompt veterinary treatment is important to relieve the allergy and prevent secondary infections in the spots where your dog opened his skin in an effort to relieve the itch.

17

All breeds are prone to certain health problems; Pit Bulls should be monitored for hip displaysia, hypothyroidism and ruptured cruciate ligament.

RINGWORM—In spite of its name, ringworm is a fungal infection, not a worm. Carried more often by cats than dogs, ringworm cause small, round, itchy bald patches, which are often inflamed because the dog cannot help but scratch them. They are easily cured by the fungicide your veterinarian will recommend.

Just as all of the aforementioned skin problems have similar symptoms, so do several others that your Pit Bull might encounter. Because it's difficult to determine exactly which condition is making your dog itch, and each one requires a different medication, leave diagnosis and treatment to your veterinarian.

CLOGGED ANAL GLANDS—If your Pit Bull is scooting along the floor on his haunches, he probably has clogged anal glands. His anal glands are located on each side of his anus, and they secrete a substance that enables your dog to pass his stool. When clogged, they are extremely uncomfortable, smell bad and could become infected. Your veterinarian can quickly unclog your dog's anal glands, or you can do it yourself if you are game. Just use one hand to hold his tail up and,

with a tissue or soft cloth in your other hand, take the skin on either side of the anus, just below the middle, in your thumb and forefinger. Then push in slightly and squeeze gently. If you succeed, a brownish, nasty-smelling substance will be on your cloth and your dog will stop scooting. Blood or pus in the secretion is a sign of infection, so if either one is present, take your Pit Bull to the veterinarian.

HIP DYSPLASIA—Hip dysplasia is caused by an abnormality of one or both hip joints. If your Pit Bull has a borderline case, it may never be noticeable to him or to you, and the only way you would know is by having his hips x-rayed. In more severe cases, hip dysplasia causes lameness in the hindquarters, ranging in severity from a slightly odd gait to inability to stand. Hip dysplasia is incurable, but there are several ways to lessen the pain, including surgery for some cases. Your veterinarian will have to x-ray your Pit Bull to determine the best treatment for him.

All dogs should be x-rayed and certified clear of hip dysplasia by the Orthopedic Foundation for Animals

(OFA) before they are used for breeding. Your veterinarian will be able to guide you through the process.

RUPTURED CRUCIATE LIGAMENT—The cruciate ligament is in the stifle joint, and its rupture is similar to the knee injury that puts many top football players on the bench. This condition is an athletic injury that will cause your Pit Bull to limp noticeably or even refuse to walk on one of the rear legs. As this injury most often sidelines heavily muscled, extremely active dogs, the Pit Bull's structure and personality combine to make him a prime candidate for the problem. In most cases, a ruptured cruciate ligament must be corrected surgically.

HYPOTHYROIDISM—The result of a hormone deficiency, hypothyroidism affects your Pit Bull's metabolism. Symptoms include a reduced activity level—in other words, less playing and more sleeping. Eventually your dog will lose interest in family fun and won't seem as bright or alert as before.

19

You can help your dog maintain good health by practicing the art of preventive care. Take good care of your Pit Bull today, and he will be healthy tomorrow.

PREVENTIVE CARE PAYS

Using common sense, paying attention to your dog and working with your veterinarian, you can minimize health risks and problems. Use vet-recommended flea, tick and heartworm preventive medications; feed a nutritious diet appropriate for your dog's size, age and activity level; give your dog sufficient exercise and regular grooming; train and socialize your dog; keep current on your dog's shots; and enjoy all the years you have with your friend.

Your Pit Bull may either gain or lose weight, and his hair will begin to dry and thin out, especially along his sides and flanks, where bald spots may occur.

Hypothyroidism is controllable in most cases, and with treatment your dog will slowly return to his alert, happy self. Your veterinarian will give him a blood test to confirm the problem and determine proper dosages of daily thyroid hormone.

CALLUSES—Dogs get calluses on their elbows and sometimes on the outsides of their hocks from sleeping on hard, rough surfaces such as concrete or gravel. The skin of the affected area becomes hairless, gray, thick and wrinkled. Usually, calluses evolve into open sores. Deep, soft bedding will prevent calluses and help keep your Pit Bull beautiful as well as comfortable.

THE IMPORTANCE OF PREVENTIVE CARE

There are many aspects of preventive care with which Pit Bull owners should be familiar: Vaccinations, regular vet visits and tooth care are just some. The advantage of preventive care is that it prevents problems.

The earlier that illness is detected in the Pit Bull, the easier it is for the veterinarian to treat the problem. Owners can help ensure their dogs' health by being on the lookout for medical problems. All this requires is an eye for detail and a willingness to observe. Pay close attention to your Pit Bull, how he looks, how he acts. What is normal behavior? How does his coat usually look? What are his eating and sleeping patterns? Subtle changes can indicate a problem. Keep close tabs on what is normal for your Pit Bull, and if anything out of the ordinary develops, call the veterinarian.

Spaying and Neutering

Spaying or neutering—surgically altering the Pit Bull so she or he cannot reproduce—should be at the top of every owner's "To Do" list. Why?

First, every day thousands of puppies are born in the United States as a result of uncontrolled breeding. For every pet living in a happy home today, there are four pets on the street or in abusive homes suffering from starvation, exposure, neglect or mistreatment. In six years, a single female dog and her offspring can be the source of 67,000 new dogs.

A second reason to spay or neuter your Pit Bull is to create a healthier, more well-adjusted pet that, in most cases, will live longer than an intact animal. A spayed female is no longer susceptible to pyometra (infection of uterus), and is less prone to mammary cancers. The procedure eliminates the behavior that accompanies the female's heat cycle. A neutered male is less likely to develop prostate or anal cancer and is less apt to roam. Marking behavior is also reduced by altering.

ADVANTAGES OF SPAYING/NEUTERING

The greatest advantage of spaying (for females) or neutering (for males) your dog is that you are guaranteed your dog will not produce puppies. There are too many puppies already available for too few homes. There are other advantages as well.

Advantages of Spaying

No messy heats.

No "suitors" howling at your windows or waiting in your yard.

No risk of pyometra (disease of the uterus) and decreased incidences of mammary cancer.

Advantages of Neutering

Decreased incidences of fighting, but does not affect the dog's personality.

Decreased roaming in search of bitches in season.

Decreased incidences of many urogenital diseases.

When should your Pit Bull be spayed or neutered? Recommendations vary among vets, but 6 months of age is commonly suggested. Ask your vet what age is best for your Pit Bull.

21

Get to know your Pit Bull's eating habits (if he starts missing meals, he may be ill).

Vaccinations

Another priority on a Pit Bull owner's list of preventive care is vaccinations. Vaccinations protect the dog against a host of infectious diseases, preventing an illness itself and the misery that accompanies it.

Vaccines should be a part of every young puppy's health care, since youngsters are so susceptible to disease. To remain effective, vaccinations must be kept current.

Good Nutrition

Dogs that receive the appropriate nutrients daily will be healthier and stronger than those that do not. The proper balance of proteins, fats, carbohydrates, vitamins, minerals and sufficient water enables the dog to remain healthy by fighting off illness.

Routine Checkups

Regular visits to the veterinary clinic should begin when your Pit Bull is a young pup and continue throughout his life. Make this a habit and it will certainly contribute to your dog's good health. Even if your Pit Bull seems perfectly healthy, a checkup once or twice a year is in order. Even if your dog seems fine to you, he could have an ongoing problem. Your veterinarian is trained to notice subtle changes or hints of illness.

Well-Being

Aside from the dog's physical needs—a proper and safe shelter, nutritious diet, health care and regular exercise—the Pit Bull needs plenty of plain, old-fashioned love. The dog is happiest when he is part of a family, enjoying the social interactions, nurturing and play. Bringing the Pit Bull into the family provides him with a sense of security.

COMMON DISEASES

Unfortunately, even with the best preventive care, the Pit Bull can fall ill. Infectious diseases, which are commonly spread from dog to dog via infected urine, feces or other body secretions, can wreak havoc. Following are a few of the diseases that can affect your pet.

Run your hands regularly over your dog to feel for any injuries.

Rabies

Probably one of the most well-known diseases that can affect dogs, rabies can strike any warm-blooded animal (including humans)—and is fatal. The rabies virus, which is present in an affected animal's saliva, is usually spread through a bite or open wound. The signs of the disease can be subtle at first. Normally friendly pets can become irritable and withdrawn. Shy pets may become overly friendly. Eventually, the dog becomes withdrawn and avoids light, which hurts the eyes of a rabid dog. Fever, vomiting and diarrhea are common.

Once these symptoms develop, the animal will die; there is no treatment or cure.

Because rabid animals may have a tendency to be aggressive and bite, animals suspected of having rabies should only be handled by animal control handlers or veterinarians.

Rabies is preventable with routine vaccines, and such vaccinations are required by law for domestic animals in all states in this country.

Parvovirus

Canine parvovirus is a highly contagious and devastating illness. The hardy virus is usually transmitted through contaminated feces, but it can be carried on an infected dog's feet or skin. It strikes dogs of all ages and is most serious in young puppies.

There are two main types of parvovirus. The first signs of the diarrhea-syndrome type are usually depression and lack of appetite,

23

YOUR PUPPY'S VACCINES

Vaccines are given to prevent your dog from getting infectious diseases like canine distemper or rabies. Vaccines are the ultimate preventive medicine: They're given before your dog ever gets the disease so as to protect him from the disease. That's why it is necessary for your dog to be vaccinated routinely. Puppy vaccines start at 8 weeks of age for the five-in-one DHLPP vaccine and are given every three to four weeks until the puppy is 16 months old. Your veterinarian will put your puppy on a proper schedule and will remind you when to bring in your dog for shots.

followed by vomiting and the characteristic bloody diarrhea. The dog appears to be in great pain, and he usually has a high fever.

The cardiac-syndrome type affects the heart muscle and is most common in young puppies. Puppies with this condition will stop nursing, whine and gasp for air. Death may occur suddenly or in a few days. Youngsters that recover can have lingering heart failure that eventually takes their life.

Veterinarians can treat dogs with parvovirus, but the outcome varies. It depends on the age of the animal and severity of the disease.

Treatment may include fluid therapy, medication to stop the severe diarrhea and antibiotics to prevent or stop secondary infection.

Young puppies receive some antibody protection against the disease from their mother, but they lose it quickly and must be vaccinated to prevent the disease. In most cases, vaccinated puppies are protected against the disease.

Coronavirus

Canine coronavirus is especially devastating to young puppies, causing depression, lack of appetite, vomiting that may contain blood and characteristically yellow-orange diarrhea. The virus is transmitted through feces, urine and saliva, and the onset of symptoms is usually rapid.

Dogs suffering from coronavirus are treated similarly to those suffering from parvovirus: fluid therapy, medication to stop diarrhea and vomiting and antibiotics if necessary.

Vaccinations are available to protect puppies and dogs against the virus and are recommended especially for those dogs in frequent contact with other dogs.

Distemper

Caused by a virus, distemper is highly contagious and is most common in unvaccinated puppies aged 3 to 8 months, but older dogs are susceptible as well. Fortunately, due to modern-day vaccines, distemper is no longer the killer it was 50 years ago.

It is especially important to vaccinate bitches before breeding to ensure maternal antibodies in the pups.

Hepatitis

Infectious canine hepatitis can affect dogs of every age, but it is most severe in puppies. It primarily affects the dog's liver, kidneys and lining of the blood vessels. Highly contagious, it is transmitted through urine, feces and saliva.

This disease has several forms. In the fatal fulminating form, the dog becomes ill very suddenly, develops bloody diarrhea and dies. In the acute form, the dog develops a fever, has bloody diarrhea, vomits blood and refuses to eat. Jaundice may be present; the whites of the dog's eyes appear yellow. Dogs with a mild case are lethargic or depressed and often refuse to eat.

Infectious canine hepatitis must be diagnosed and confirmed with a blood test. Ill dogs require hospitalization. Hepatitis is preventable in dogs by keeping vaccinations current.

Lyme Disease

Lyme disease has received a lot of press recently, with its increased incidence throughout the United States. The illness, caused by the bacteria *Borrelia burgdorferi,* is carried by ticks. It is passed along when the tick bites a victim, canine or human. (The dog cannot pass the disease to people, though. It is only transmitted via the tick.) It is most common during the tick season in May through August.

In dogs, the disease manifests itself in sudden lameness, caused by swollen joints, similar to arthritis. The dog is weak and may run a fever. The lameness can last a few days or several months, and some dogs have recurring difficulties.

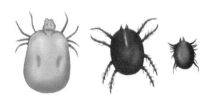

Three types of ticks (l-r): the wood tick, brown dog tick and deer tick.

Use tweezers to remove ticks from your dog.

Antibiotics are very effective in treating Lyme disease, and the sooner it is diagnosed and treated, the better. A vaccine is available; ask your veterinarian if your dog would benefit from it.

Kennel Cough

"Kennel cough," or the more politically correct "canine cough," shows itself as a harsh, dry cough. This contagious disease has been termed "kennel cough," much to the dismay of kennel owners, because of its often rapid spread through kennels. The cough may persist for weeks and is often followed by a bout of chronic bronchitis.

Many kennels require proof of bordatella vaccination before boarding. If your dog is in and out of kennels frequently, vaccination certainly is not a bad idea.

FIRST AID

First aid is not a substitute for professional care, though it can help save a dog's life.

To Stop Bleeding

Bleeding from a severe cut or wound must be stopped right away. There are two basic techniques—direct pressure and the tourniquet.

Try to control bleeding first by using direct pressure. Ask an assistant to hold the injured Pit Bull and place several pads of sterile gauze over the wound. Press. Do not wipe the wound or apply any cleansers or ointments. Apply firm, even pressure. If blood soaks through the pad, do not remove it as this could disrupt clotting. Simply place another pad on top and continue to apply pressure.

If bleeding on a leg or the tail does not stop by applying pressure, try using a tourniquet. Use this only as a last resort. A tourniquet that is left on too long can result in limb loss.

If the dog is bleeding from his mouth or anus, or vomits or defecates blood, he may be suffering from internal injuries. Do not attempt to stop bleeding. Call the veterinarian right away for emergency treatment.

Shock

Whenever a dog is injured or is seriously ill, the odds are good that he will go into a state of shock. A decreased supply of oxygen to the tissues usually results in unconsciousness, pale gums, weak, rapid pulse and labored, rapid breathing. If not treated, a dog will die from shock. The conditions of the dog should continue to be treated, but the dog should be as comfortable as possible. A blanket can help keep a dog warm. A dog in shock needs immediate veterinary care.

Poisoning

A dog's curiosity will often lead him to eat or lick things he shouldn't. Unfortunately, many substances are poisonous to dogs, including

POISON ALERT

If your dog has ingested a potentially poisonous substance, waste no time. Call the National Animal Poison Control Center hot line:

(800) 548-2423 ($30 per case) or

(900) 680-0000 ($20 first five minutes; $2.95 each additional minute)

Some of the many household substances harmful to your dog.

27

household products, plants or chemicals. Owners must learn to act quickly if poisoning is suspected because the results can be deadly.

If your dog appears to be poisoned:

- Call your veterinarian and follow his or her directions.

- Try to identify the poison source—this is really important. Take the container or plant to the clinic.

WHEN TO CALL THE VETERINARIAN

In any emergency situation, you should call your veterinarian immediately. Try to stay calm when you call, and give the vet or the assistant as much information as possible before you leave for the clinic. That way, the staff will be able to take immediate, specific action when you arrive. Emergencies include:

- Bleeding or deep wounds
- Hyperthermia (overheating)
- Shock
- Dehydration
- Abdominal pain
- Burns
- Fits
- Unconsciousness
- Broken bones
- Paralysis

Call your veterinarian if you suspect any health troubles.

Heatstroke

Heatstroke can be deadly and must be treated immediately to save the dog. Signs include rapid panting, darker-than-usual gums and tongue, salivating, exhaustion or vomiting.

The dog's body temperature is elevated, sometimes as high as 106°F. If the dog is not treated, coma and death can follow.

If heatstroke is suspected, cool down your overheated dog as quickly as possible and call your veterinarian. Mildly affected dogs can be moved to a cooler environment, into an air-conditioned home, for example, or wrapped in moistened towels.

Insect Bites/Stings

Just like people, dogs can suffer bee stings and insect bites. Bees, wasps and yellow jackets leave a nasty, painful sting, and if your dog is stung repeatedly shock can occur.

If an insect bite is suspected, try to identify the culprit. Remove the stinger if it is a bee sting, and apply a mixture of baking soda and water to the sting. It is also a good idea to apply ice packs to reduce inflammation and ease pain. Call your veterinarian, especially if your dog seems ill or goes into shock.

INTERNAL PARASITES

Dogs are susceptible to several internal parasites. Keeping your Pit Bull free of internal parasites is another important aspect of health care.

Watch for general signs of poor condition: a dull coat, weight loss, lethargy, coughing, weakness and diarrhea.

For proper diagnosis and treatment of internal parasites, consult a veterinarian.

Roundworms

Roundworms, or ascarids, are probably the most common worms that affect dogs. Most puppies are born with these organisms in their intestines, which is why youngsters are treated for these parasites as soon as it is safe to do so.

Animals contract roundworms by ingesting infected soil and feces. A roundworm infestation can rob vital nutrients from young puppies and cause diarrhea, vomiting and digestive upset. Roundworms can also harm a young animal's liver and lungs, so treatment is imperative.

Tapeworms

Tapeworms are commonly transmitted by fleas to dogs. Tapeworm eggs enter the body of a canine host when the animal accidentally ingests a carrier flea. The parasite settles in

the intestines, where it sinks its head into the intestinal wall and feeds off material the host is digesting. The worm grows a body of egg packets, which break off periodically and are expelled from the body in the feces. Fleas then ingest the eggs from the feces and the parasite's life cycle begins all over again.

Hookworms

Hookworms are so named because they hook onto an animal's small intestine and suck the host's blood. Like roundworms, hookworms are contracted when a dog ingests contaminated soil or feces.

Hookworms can be especially devastating to dogs. They will become thin and sick; puppies can die. An affected dog will suffer from bloody diarrhea and, if the parasites migrate to the lungs, the dog may contract bronchitis or pneumonia.

Hookworms commonly strike puppies 2 to 8 weeks of age and are less common in adult dogs.

Whipworms

Known for their thread-like appearance, whipworms attach into the wall of the large intestine to feed. Thick-shelled eggs are passed in the

WHAT'S WRONG WITH MY DOG?

We've listed some common conditions of health problems and their possible causes. If any of the following conditions appear serious or persist for more than 24 hours, make an appointment to see your veterinarian immediately.

CONDITIONS	POSSIBLE CAUSES
DIARRHEA	Intestinal upset, typically caused by eating something bad or overeating. Can also be a viral infection, a bad case of nerves or anxiety or a parasite infection. If you see blood in the feces, get to the vet right away.
VOMITING/RETCHING	Dogs regurgitate fairly regularly (bitches for their young) whenever something upsets their stomach, or even out of excitement or anxiety. Often dogs eat grass, which, because it's indigestible in its pure form, irritates their stomachs and causes them to vomit. Getting a good look at *what* your dog vomited can better indicate what's causing it.
COUGHING	Obstruction in the throat; virus (kennel cough); roundworm infestation; congestive heart failure.
RUNNY NOSE	Because dogs don't catch colds like people, a runny nose is a sign of congestion or irritation.
LOSS OF APPETITE	Because most dogs are hearty and regular eaters, a loss of appetite can be your first and most accurate sign of a serious problem.
LOSS OF ENERGY (LETHARGY)	Any number of things could be slowing down your dog, from an infection to internal tumors to overexercise—even overeating.

feces and in about two to four weeks are mature and able to reinfect a host that ingests the eggs.

Mild whipworm infestation is often without signs, but as the worms grow, weight loss, bloody diarrhea and anemia follow. In areas where the soil is heavily contaminated, frequent checks are advised to prevent severe infestation.

CONDITIONS	POSSIBLE CAUSES
STINKY BREATH	Imagine if you never brushed your teeth! Foul-smelling breath indicates plaque and tartar buildup that could possibly have caused infection. Start brushing your dog's teeth.
LIMPING	This could be caused by something as simple as a hurt or bruised pad, to something as complicated as hip dysplasia, torn ligaments or broken bones.
CONSTANT ITCHING	Probably due to fleas, mites or an allergic reaction to food or environment (your vet will need to help you determine what your dog's allergic to).
RED, INFLAMED, ITCHY SPOTS	Often referred to as "hot spots," these are particularly common on coated breeds. They're caused by a bacterial infection that gets aggravated as the dog licks and bites at the spot.
BALD SPOTS	These are the result of excessive itching or biting at the skin so that the hair follicles are damaged; excessively dry skin; mange; calluses; and even infections. You need to determine what the underlying cause is.
STINKY EARS/HEAD SHAKING	Take a look under your dog's ear flap. Do you see brown, waxy buildup? Clean the ears with something soft and a special cleaner, and don't use cotton swabs or go too deep into the ear canal.
UNUSUAL LUMPS	Could be fatty tissue, could be something serious (infection, trauma, tumor). Don't wait to find out.

31

Heartworms

Heartworm larvae are transmitted by the ordinary mosquito, but the effects are far from ordinary. In three to four months, the larvae (microfilaria) become small worms and make their way to a vein, where they are transported to the heart, where they grow and reproduce.

FLEAS AND TICKS

There are so many safe, effective products available now to combat fleas and ticks that—thankfully—they are less of a problem. Prevention is key, however. Ask your veterinarian about starting your puppy on a flea/tick repellent right away. With this, regular grooming and environmental controls, your dog and your home should stay pest-free. Without this attention, you risk infesting your dog and your home, and you're in for an ugly and costly battle to clear up the problem.

At first, a dog with heartworms is free of symptoms. The signs vary, but the most common is a deep cough and shortness of breath. The dog tires easily, is weak and loses weight. Eventually, the dog may suffer from congestive heart failure.

EXTERNAL PARASITES

FLEAS—Besides carrying tapeworm larvae, fleas bite and suck the host's blood. Their bites itch and are extremely annoying to dogs, especially if the dog is hypersensitive to the bite. Fleas must be eliminated on the dog with special shampoos and dips. Fleas also infest the dog's bedding and the owner's home and yard.

TICKS—Several varieties of ticks attach themselves to dogs, where they burrow into the skin and suck blood. Ticks can be carriers of several diseases, including Lyme disease and Rocky Mountain Spotted Fever.

LICE—Lice are not common in dogs, but when they are present they cause intense irritation and itching. There are two types: biting and sucking. Biting lice feed on skin scales, and sucking lice feed on blood.

MITES—There are several types of mites that cause several kinds of mange, including sarcoptic, demodectic and cheyletiella. These microscopic mites cause intense itching and misery to the dog.

Positively Nutritious

The nutritional needs of a dog will change throughout her lifetime. It is necessary to be aware of these changes not only for proper initial growth to occur, but also so your dog can lead a healthy life for many years.

Before bringing your puppy home, ask the breeder for the puppy's feeding schedule and information about what and how much she is used to eating. Maintain this regimen for at least the first few

HOW TO READ
THE DOG FOOD LABEL

With so many choices on the market, how can you be sure you are feeding the right food to your dog? The information is all there on the label—if you know what you're looking for.

Look for the nutritional claim right up top. Is the food "100 percent nutritionally complete"? If so, it's for nearly all life stages; "growth and maintenance," on the other hand, is for early development; puppy foods are marked as such, as are foods for senior dogs.

Ingredients are listed in descending order by weight. The first three or four ingredients will tell you the bulk of what the food contains. Look for the highest-quality ingredients, like meats and grains, to be among them.

The Guaranteed Analysis tells you what levels of protein, fat, fiber and moisture are in the food, in that order. While these numbers are meaningful, they won't tell you much about the quality of the food. Nutritional value is in the dry matter, not the moisture content.

In many ways, seeing is believing. If your dog has bright eyes, a shiny coat, a good appetite and a good energy level, chances are her diet's fine. Your dog's breeder and your veterinarian are good sources of advice if you're still confused.

days before gradually changing to a schedule that is more in line with the family's lifestyle. The breeder may supply you with a small quantity of the food the puppy has been eating. Use this or have your own supply of the same food ready when you bring home your puppy.

After the puppy has been with you for three days and has become acclimated to her new environment, you can begin a gradual food change. Progressively substitute a little more of the new food each day until it has entirely replaced the previous diet. This gradual change will prevent an upset stomach and diarrhea. The total amount of food to be fed at each meal will progressively increase from day to day at this stage of the puppy's life.

LIFE-STAGE
FEEDING

Puppies and adolescent dogs require a much higher intake of protein, calories and nutrients than adult dogs due to the demands of their rapidly developing bodies. Most commercial brands of dry kibble meet these requirements and are

34

well balanced for proper growth. The majority of puppy foods now available are so carefully planned that it is unwise to attempt to add anything other than water to them.

The major ingredients of most dry dog foods are chicken, beef or lamb by-products and corn, wheat or rice. The higher the meat content, the higher the protein percentage, palatability and digestibility of the food. Protein percentages in puppy food are usually between 25 and 30 percent. There are many advantages of dry foods over semimoist and canned dog foods for puppies and normal, healthy adult Pit Bulls.

It is best to feed meals that are primarily dry food because the chewing action involved in eating a dry food is better for the health of the teeth and gums. Dry food is also less expensive than canned food of equal quality.

Dogs whose diets are based on canned or soft foods have a greater likelihood of developing calcium deposits and gum disease. Canned or semimoist foods do serve certain functions, however. As a supplement to dry dog food, in small portions, canned or semimoist foods can be

FOOD ALLERGIES

If your puppy or dog seems to itch all the time for no apparent reason, she could be allergic to one or more ingredients in her food. This is not uncommon, and it's why many foods contain lamb and rice instead of beef, wheat or soy. Have your dog tested by your veterinarian, and be patient while you strive to identify and eliminate the allergens from your dog's food (or environment).

Puppies and adolescent dogs require a high intake of protein, calories and other nutrients to fuel their rapidly developing bodies.

35

useful to stimulate appetites and aid in weight gain. But unless very special conditions exist, they are not the

Feeding your Pit Bull dry food helps keep her teeth and gums healthy.

Feeding your Pit Bull table scraps encourages bad manners.

best way for a dog to meet her nutritional needs.

DIFFERENT DOGS NEED DIFFERENT DIETS

There has been considerable research over the past few years to suggest that nutrient requirements change according to age, condition, activity level, gestation, lactation and so on, and this only makes sense on an intuitive level. A dog who runs hundreds of miles a week hunting is going to burn more calories than a Pit Bull couch potato.

While the protein requirements may not change that much, the energy difference must come either from additional carbohydrates or from fat. Fat has more calories on a dry-weight basis than either protein or carbohydrates, so it is the logical choice for supplementing the diets of hardworking animals.

Advances in feed manufacturing techniques have made it possible to incorporate higher levels of fat into extruded dog foods than in the past, thereby eliminating the need for the dog owner to add it on after the fact, which used to throw the correct nutritional proportions out of balance.

HOW MUCH TO FEED?

If you take the recommendation of the breeder in selecting the food, keep in mind that the amounts they feed are based on the activity levels of their dogs in their geographical area. Similarly, the recommended feeding quantities as they appear on the bag are guidelines. Some Pit

GROWTH STAGE FOODS

Once upon a time, there was puppy food and there was adult dog food. Now there are foods for puppies, young adults/active dogs, less active dogs and senior citizens. What's the difference between these foods? They vary by the amounts of nutrients they provide for the dog's growth stage/activity level.

Less active dogs don't need as much protein or fat as growing, active dogs; senior dogs don't need some of the nutrients vital to puppies. By feeding a high-quality food that's appropriate for your dog's age and activity level, you're benefiting your dog and yourself. Feed too much protein to a couch potato and she'll have energy to spare, which means a few more trips around the block will be needed to burn it off. Feed an adult diet to a puppy, and risk growth and development abnormalities that could affect her for a lifetime.

Bulls will get fat on one cup of premium food a day, and another might require twice that just to keep her ribs from showing. This means you will have to use your own judgment after getting input from the vet, breeder and feed store.

How Many Meals a Day?

Individual dogs vary in how much they should eat to maintain a desired body weight—not too fat, but not too thin. Puppies need several meals a day, while older dogs may need only one. Determine how much food keeps your adult dog looking and feeling her best. Then decide how many meals you want to feed with that amount. Like us, most dogs love to eat, and offering two meals a day is more enjoyable for them. If you're worried about overfeeding, make sure you measure correctly and abstain from adding tidbits to the meals.

Whether you feed one or two meals, only leave your dog's food out for the amount of time it takes her to eat it—ten minutes, for example. Free-feeding (when food is available any time) and leisurely meals encourage picky eating. Don't worry if your dog doesn't finish all her dinner in the allotted time. She'll learn she should.

A well-fed Pit Bull will always be a bit hungry, so that is not a clue as to the proper amount to feed. The rule of thumb as to whether your Pit Bull is the correct weight is that you should be able to feel her ribs but not see them. If she is free of parasites and kept reasonably clean, there should be a "bloom" on her coat that comes with just the right amount of subcutaneous fat.

Should you feed the meal wet or dry? There are pluses and minuses to each method, and you will have to determine what works best for you and your Pit Bull. Feeding wet usually means either moistening or soaking the dry food in warm water or broth for a few minutes. This method is recommended for young puppies, whose dentition may not be up to crunching down their meals easily. Advocates of wet feeding believe it results in less bloating. It may also increase palatability and digestibility—considerations more important for puppies than for adults.

Dry feeding requires no time delay and may help slow down a dog who would otherwise gulp down her food. It may also be better for your pet's dental health. Also, on those rare occasions when your pet doesn't immediately clean her plate, you needn't be concerned with spoilage.

*Like humans,
Pit Bulls need
plenty of exer-
cise and a
nutritious diet
to keep fit and
healthy.*

39

*Your Pit Bull
may require
additional calo-
ries if she is very
active.*

Putting on the Dog

your dog clean and shiny, but you will accomplish much more than that. Grooming feels good to you and your dog and will strengthen the bond between you. Inspecting your Pit Bull for external parasites, minor injuries and early signs of skin disease while grooming helps you find and solve small problems before they become big, expensive ones.

There are few jobs more difficult than trimming the nails of a mature, 50-pound Pit Bull who is not accustomed to having his feet touched. But if you condition your dog from puppyhood to accept grooming as a regular part of life, he will soon learn that being handled and brushed is pleasant. By the time he

Grooming your Pit Bull will soon become a pleasant, relaxing part of your daily routine. It takes less than five minutes a day to keep

Grooming your Pit Bull from puppyhood will make him more cooperative as an adult.

is half-grown, he should be steady and cooperative when you groom him.

BRUSHING

Daily brushing will make your Pit Bull sparkle because brushing removes dander, dirt and dead hair, while stimulating the secretion of natural oils that keep his coat sleek and shiny. Two types of brushes will be effective on your dog. The first (and the one you will use most often) can be a hand-held brush with medium-soft bristles or a glove type of brush, which usually has horsehair bristles. Brush his coat gently but firmly in the direction of growth. When no more loose hair or dander comes out and his coat gleams, you have brushed enough. To groom his face, use a damp cloth instead of a brush.

Your second brush should be a rubber curry brush of about palm size, useful after your dog has a romp in the mud. When you can actually see the dirt on his coat, use the curry before using your regular brush. Let the mud dry before you curry, and then curry by moving the

Keep your Pit Bull's coat healthy by brushing him every day.

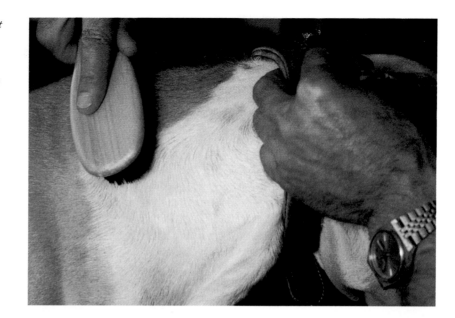

While you are grooming your Pit Bull, inspect him for wounds, skin problems, parasites and anything else that seems out of the ordinary.

rubber brush in small circles all over the upper part of his body. Skip his legs, feet, belly and face (and the genitals on a male), as the curry is too rough for those areas. Your regular brush will easily remove mud from your Pit Bull's legs and feet, and a damp cloth will clean his nearly bald belly and his face (and a male's genital area).

Inspect your dog while brushing him. Look for open wounds that need washing and treatment, signs of skin disease, external parasites and bumps, warts, splinters or anything else that could signal the start of a problem.

TEETH AND TOENAILS

To check your Pit Bull's teeth for tartar, hold his head firmly and lift his lips upward. A soft toothbrush or damp washcloth dipped in baking soda usually removes discoloration on the teeth. If the stains are not easily removed, ask your veterinarian if your dog's teeth need a professional cleaning. Hard dog biscuits and nylon chew toys will help keep a young dog's teeth white, but are not enough to do the whole job.

Your Pit Bull's toenails are too long if they make clicking noises on the floor when he walks or touch the ground when he is standing still. Dogs with very long nails tend to walk on the back of their feet, leading to splayed toes and an unattractive gait. Not only is this uncomfortable for the dog, but there is an additional danger. If untrimmed, toenails and dewclaws eventually curl under the foot, circling back to puncture the pads.

To clip your Pit Bull's nails, lift his foot up and forward. Hold it securely in one hand, allowing your dominant hand to do the trimming. If your dog has white nails, your job is easier than if his nails are dark. There is a blood vessel called the quick in the bottom stem of the

43

Check your dog's teeth by holding his head securely and lifting his lips upward.

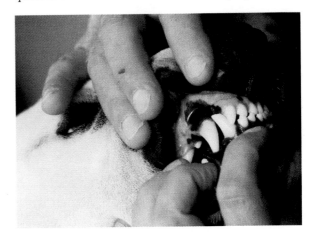

QUICK AND PAINLESS NAIL CLIPPING

This is possible if you make a habit out of handling your dog's feet and giving your dog treats when you do. When it's time to clip nails, go through the same routine, but take your clippers and snip off just the ends of the nail—clip too far down and you'll cut into the "quick," the nerve center, hurting your dog and causing the nail to bleed. Clip two nails a session while you're getting your dog used to the procedure, and you'll soon be doing all four feet quickly and easily.

44

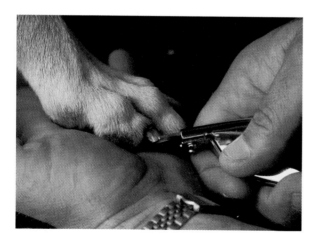

Trim your Pit Bull's nails in small increments, clipping just outside the quick.

like projection on the underside of the nail.

When you cut the nail properly, your dog will feel nothing more than slight pressure, the same as you feel when cutting your own toenails. If you accidentally cut the quick, the nail will hurt and bleed. Stop the bleeding with a styptic pencil or powder sold at pet supply stores. Pressing the bleeding nail into a soft bar of soap for a minute or so will also stop the bleeding. Try to work under good lighting so you can cut your dog's nails without a mishap. He will forgive a cut quick if it is a rare occurrence, but if you are clumsy too often, he may begin to resist work on his feet.

BATHING

Because brushing cleans the coat and reduces body odors, your Pit Bull will rarely need a bath if he gets three to five minutes of brushing daily. Bathe him only when necessary, because shampooing dries the coat by washing away natural oils.

Equipment for a bath includes old clothes (when your dog shakes, you'll be as wet as he is); a tub, preferably with a drain so he won't be standing in soapy water; a rubber

nail, which is clearly seen through white nails. Trim the nail just outside the quick. You will not be able to see the quick in dark nails, so make the cut just outside the hook-

mat for traction in the tub; a spray-nozzle hose attachment or a pail for dipping water; pH-balanced dog shampoo or insecticide shampoo (and a flea-and-tick dip if necessary); cotton balls; a washcloth; mineral oil; and a large towel or two. Coat conditioner applied after the shampoo is optional.

Before bathing your Pit Bull, allow him to exercise outside for a few minutes. That way he won't have to dash outdoors to relieve himself (and probably roll in the loose garden dirt) immediately following his bath.

The bath water should be warm but not hot. Begin by placing a cotton ball inside each of his ears, to keep the water out. Next, spray or pour water over his whole body with the exception of his face and head. Put a small amount of shampoo on his back and massage the lather well into his coat. Then add more shampoo as needed to clean his legs, neck, tail and underbelly. If you accidentally get soap in your dog's eyes, put a few drops of mineral oil in the inner corner of each eye to relieve the sting. Use the hose or pail to thoroughly rinse off the lather. Do not rush this step. Shampoo left to dry in the coat makes it dull

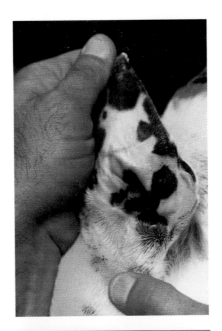

Take care to protect your Pit Bull's ears and eyes during his bath; place a cotton ball in each ear to keep water out, and use a few drops of mineral oil in the corner of each eye to relieve irritation caused by soap.

45

Grooming brings out the sparkle of a healthy, well-cared-for dog.

his ears and wipe them out with a dry cotton ball dipped in a bit of mineral oil. Then wrap him in a towel, lift him from the tub, and towel-dry him well, especially his chest and underbelly.

THE INSIDE OUTS OF GOOD LOOKS

Good grooming is no substitute for poor health or lack of physical fitness. Good looks start from within, with quality food, regular exercise, clean housing and no internal or external parasites. Health problems sometimes first show themselves through a dry, brittle coat lacking in luster. Pit Bulls in good condition sparkle from the inside out, and regular grooming sessions simply bring the healthy glow to the surface.

and can cause intense itching. If you are using insecticide shampoo or dip, follow the label's directions carefully.

Finish by wiping his face and head with a warm, well-wrung washcloth. Remove the cotton from

Measuring Up

The Pit Bull is a fit and handsome medium-size dog with a muscular body, sleek coat, comical expressions and an affectionate nature. Considered the strongest dog in the world for its size, for many years it was one of the most respected and beloved breeds in our nation.

Studying the breed standard is the best way to learn the distinguishing characteristics of a breed. The following is the standard of the Pit Bull as approved by the United Kennel Club (UKC) in January 1978. The official standard is printed in italics, and explanations and comments are in regular type. Remember, the UKC standard explains only the breed's appearance.

The breed's temperament is of far greater importance and is discussed in other chapters.

It is important to keep in mind when reading the standard and

WHAT IS A BREED STANDARD?

Abreed standard—a detailed description of an individual breed—is meant to portray the ideal specimen of that breed. This includes ideal structure, temperament, gait, type—all aspects of the dog. Because the standard describes an ideal specimen, it isn't based on any particular dog. It is a concept against which judges compare actual dogs and breeders strive to produce dogs. At a dog show, the dog that wins is the one that comes closest, in the judge's opinion, to the standard for its breed. Breed standards are written by the breed parent clubs, the national organizations formed to oversee the well-being of the breed. They are voted on and approved by the members of the parent clubs.

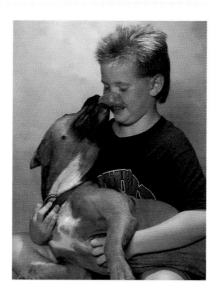

Regardless of how close your Pit Bull comes to the breed standard, she's still a great pet.

trying to match one's own Pit Bull to it that the standard describes an ideal Pit Bull, and some sections are geared toward a show interpretation.

PIT BULL STANDARD OF THE UNITED KENNEL CLUB

HEAD—*Medium length. Bricklike in shape. Skull flat and widest at the ears, with prominent cheeks free from wrinkles.*

The head gives the first impression of the dog. The skull is large and rather square, combining width and depth. The cheek muscles are well-defined, and the skin fits smoothly over the protruding muscle with no excess to droop or wrinkle. Though blocky and broad, the head's classic chiseled appearance, packed with bulging muscle, combines character and strength.

MUZZLE—*Square, wide and deep. Well-pronounced jaws, displaying strength. Upper teeth should meet tightly over lower teeth, outside in front.*

The jaw should appear strong and bold with the underjaw very evident so the muzzle can end in an impression of squareness. If the underjaw is weakly formed or receding, the muzzle will appear to be pointy in profile instead of square, and will also seem longer than it actually is. A weak muzzle lacks the characteristic look of power and is termed "snipy."

Sometimes a well-formed, squarish jaw is disguised because a dog has heavy, hanging upper lips. Pendulous upper lips hide the clean lines of the muzzle by falling below the lower jaw. Such lips were a distinct disadvantage in the warrior dogs of old and are still considered undesirable. The tighter the lips fit on a Pit Bull, the better.

When the upper front teeth meet tightly outside the lower front teeth, the dog has a scissors bite. It is the best gripping as well as the strongest bite, and is considered ideal. There are three types of less-than-perfect bites. One is the undershot mouth, where the lower jaw protrudes so that the lower front teeth (incisors) close in front of the upper incisors. Another is the overshot mouth, in which the upper jaw protrudes so there is a space or gap between the upper and lower incisors when the mouth is closed. More rare is the wry bite, a scissors

This dog proudly sports the weight-pulling harness he wears to do his job.

49

bite on one side but undershot on the other side. Dogs with slightly faulty bites have no trouble eating. Most incorrect bites are a cosmetic fault, not a functional problem.

EARS—*Cropped or uncropped (not important). Should be set high on head, and be free from wrinkles.*

Cropped ears are trimmed in an attractive, prick-eared style. Uncropped ears are simply the natural ears with which the dog was born. Both cropped and natural ears should add to the Pit Bull's animated expression by alerting to stimuli.

The most attractive natural ears are fairly small and are rose or half-prick. Rose ears have a backward fold allowing a bit of the burr (inner ear) to show. The tips of rose ears usually point toward the side, but they may also point toward the back of the dog's head, depending on their size, formation and whether or not the dog is responding to stimuli or resting. Generally the tips move forward and point sideways when the dog is alert and lie toward the back when the dog relaxes.

Half-pricked ears start upward and then fold over toward the front about halfway up. Sometimes the tips hang slightly to the sides of the dog's head, but they are always closer to the front than rose ears.

Some Pit Bulls have half-pricked ears that start upward and then fold over halfway.

Like rose ears, half-pricked ears also look nice when they are on the small side.

An occasional Pit Bull has full drop ears of the type seen on retrievers and spaniels. Such ears are not typical of the breed and add nothing in the way of animation to a dog's expression, but function just as well as any other ear.

EYES—*Round. Should be set far apart, low down on skull. Any color acceptable.*

Closely set eyes are a cosmetic fault that tend to make a dog look crafty and sly rather than intelligent. They also make the muzzle appear too narrow and too long, robbing the dog of the bold expression that is so much a part of this breed.

When the outside corner of the eye is in line with the indentation seen directly over the beginning of the cheek muscle, the eyes are set at the most attractive height in relation to the skull.

NOSE—*Wide-open nostrils. Any color acceptable.*

NECK—*Muscular. Slightly arched. Tapering from shoulder to head. Free from looseness of skin.*

The neck should be well-muscled and appear strong. This is especially important along the top, where good musculature accentuates an attractively arched neck. The neck should be narrowest just behind the ears and widen downward gradually to blend smoothly into the withers (top of the shoulders).

Clean lines and tightly fitting skin are desirable in the Pit Bull. Wrinkles of loose skin under a dog's throat are termed "throatiness" or "having a dewlap" and are a cosmetic fault.

SHOULDERS—*Strong and muscular, with wide, sloping shoulder blades.*

Good shoulder blades are wide and well-covered with muscle. "Sloping shoulder blades" means that the shoulder blade or scapula should have a very evident backward slope from its lower end (at the dog's upper arm) to its higher end (just in front of the withers). Shoulders with the proper slope are often termed "well laid back."

A long, well-angulated (properly sloping) blade, with muscle well distributed over the shoulder area helps the dog have ample reach with his front legs and gives the dog attractive flowing lines.

BACK—*Short and strong. Slightly sloping from withers to rump. Slightly arched at loins, which should be slightly tucked.*

A Pit Bull with good proportions between length and height is a rather square dog. This means if you measure her from the point of the shoulder to the point of the buttock, and then from the withers to the ground, the two measurements should be close to the same. An overly long back makes a dog too long in proportion to her height, and the excess length usually shows up in the loin, giving the dog's back an aspect of weakness rather than strength.

The dog's topline (the top of the back from the withers to where the tail begins) *should flow smoothly without wrinkles of loose skin or rolls of fat.* The topline should be slightly higher at the withers than the rump, with a subtle arch just over the loin area.

The loin area is the dog's waistline and should have a noticeable indentation when seen from above. It should not be so slim, however, that it makes the dog appear weak. The indentation should be just enough to give the body shape, so it does not look like a log or a plump sausage.

The Pit Bull's proportions make her look like a square dog.

CHEST—*Deep, but not too broad, with wide-sprung ribs.*

The Pit Bull should have enough space between her front legs to make room for a well-developed forechest (also called the brisket). The forechest is the front part of the dog's chest. As it goes down between the front legs to meet the chest, the forechest should be deep enough at its lowest point to be even with the dog's elbow when viewed from the side. This does not mean that wider is better with regard to the space between a dog's front legs or the width of the forechest. An overly broad front is coarse and

bulldogish, making for a less agile animal. No feature of the dog should dominate her other features. In the most attractive Pit Bulls, every part is in perfect proportion to every other part. This results in a balanced, athletic animal.

RIBS—*Close. Well-sprung, with deep-back ribs.*

When a Pit Bull's well-sprung rib cage continues far back toward the dog's rear quarters, the back is considered "well-ribbed," or "deep in the rear." This is important because deep-back ribs allow more room for lung expansion during exercise, giving the dog more physical staying power.

TAIL—*Short in comparison to size. Set low and tapering to a fine point. Not carried over back. Bobbed tail not acceptable.*

The tail is important because it is a continuation of the spinal column. A tail that is noticeably thin and weak, or a kinked or crooked tail, could indicate a similar defect in the spine.

The ideal tail for a Pit Bull resembles an old-fashioned pump handle. It should begin with a strong, thick root and taper to a point that ends even with, or a little above, the hock point. The set on of the tail (where the root emerges from the dog's body) should be rather low, although not as low as the tail set of some racing breeds.

When the Pit Bull is moving, her tail should not be carried any higher than the top of her back.

LEGS—*Large, round-boned, with straight, upright pasterns, reasonably strong. Feet to be of medium size. Gait should be light and springy. No rolling or pacing.*

The leg bones should be large enough in circumference to appear to support the weight of the dog easily.

The Pit Bull's front legs should be straight and sturdy. The feet should point directly front, not toward each other (toed in) or away from each other. The lowest part of the front leg, from the joint just above the foot down to the foot, is called the pastern. It should stand erect and appear strong.

The Pit Bull's gait should appear effortless. The dog should move forward boldly, with a jaunty, self-confident attitude and no wasted

motion. When the dog trots, her topline should move smoothly. The trot is a diagonal gait with the left front and the right rear legs moving forward together, followed by the right front and the left rear.

THIGH—*Long, with muscles developed. Hocks down and straight.*

The rear leg has an upper thigh and a lower thigh, separated by the stifle (knee joint), located on the frontal portion of the dog's hind leg. Both thighs should appear strong and be covered by hard muscle.

The hock joint is the joint between the stifle and the foot. "Hocks down" means that the hock should be located much lower than the middle of the dog's rear leg, rather close to the ground.

When watched from the rear, the dog's back legs should appear parallel. Hocks turning either toward each other or away from each other are faulty.

COAT—*Glossy. Short and stiff to the touch.*

A dog's coat gives evidence of the general health of the dog, and a Pit Bull in good condition usually has a beautiful, shiny coat. The hair

53

Any color or marking is acceptable for your Pit Bull.

should be rather coarse in texture, which provides the best protection in a short coat.

COLOR—*Any color or marking permissible.*

WEIGHT—*Not important. Females preferred from 30 to 50 pounds. Males from 35 to 60 pounds.*

The Pit Bull's height and weight should be in proportion.

AMERICAN DOG BREEDERS ASSOCIATION STANDARD

The American Dog Breeders Association (ADBA) also offers a standard for the Pit Bull. The explanation of each item in the standard is part of the document. To obtain a copy, write to the American Dog Breeders Association, Inc., Box 1771, Salt Lake City, UT 84110.

A Matter of Fact

Archaeologists agree that dogs were the first animals domesticated by man. Cave drawings from the Paleolithic era, the earliest part of the Old World Stone Age (50,000 years ago), show men and dogs hunting together. Gradually, man found additional uses for dogs. The earliest known ancestors of the Pit Bull served as guards and draft animals, but they were especially esteemed as dogs of war.

ORIGIN OF THE PIT BULL

The ancient Greeks had huge, ferocious dogs of a type called Mollossian, which historians believe originated in Asia. During the sixth century B.C., Phoenician traders brought some of these Greek guard dogs to England. There they flourished and became the ancestors of England's early mastiff-type dogs.

When the Roman Legions invaded Britain, they were met on the beaches by the Britons' fierce mastiff-type war dogs fighting side by side with their owners. The Romans admired these fighting dogs so much that they sent many of them home to Italy. There the dogs were called Pugnaces, or the broad-mouthed dogs of Britain. As the Roman legions spread across Europe, so did the dogs.

Warrior dogs also starred in the bloody Roman circuses, where they were used to fight savage animals of other species, armed men and each other. Around A.D. 395, the Roman historian Symmachus wrote about seven Irish bulldogs who excited a circus audience with their savage fighting and brave attitude.

Early ancestors of Pit Bulls were used as guard and warrior dogs.

Symmachus called the deadly dogs bulldogs, because dogs of that type were used to fight bulls.

THE ANCIENT BULLDOG

During ancient times there were no breeds as we know breeds today, and dogs were usually named for the work they did. For example, in England all guard dogs of massive size were considered mastiffs, and all dogs quick, brave and small enough to enter a hole in the ground (terra) after wild game, such as badgers or foxes, were called terriers.

Eventually, some of the mastiff-type dogs became specialists. A 1632 dictionary defined the Alaunt as a mastiff-like dog used by the British butchers to round up and pen fierce oxen. The Bandog was any large guard dog who was kept chained by day. And the Bulldog, of course, was the gladiator.

THE BLOOD SPORTS

Blood sports were so much a part of daily life in England that around 1800, in the town of Wednesbury in Staffordshire County, church bells

The Pit Bull's amazing strength is demonstrated at weight pull competitions like this one.

rang in celebration of "Old Sal," when she finally managed to have puppies. Sal was famous for gameness but had never been able to whelp a litter. If a Bulldog bitch died during whelping in that mining district, women often raised the puppies by suckling them at their own breasts.

Bullbaiting and other blood sports were not just entertainment for the working classes, but for all classes. In fact, kings and queens often mandated that a contest be arranged. When French ambassadors visited the court of Queen Elizabeth in 1559, the Queen graciously entertained them with a fine dinner followed by an exhibition of dogs baiting bulls and bears.

King James I continued Queen Elizabeth's tradition by having a special baiting arranged to entertain ambassadors from the Spanish Court. His son, King Charles I, was also an avid spectator of blood sports, and during the days of Queen Anne (1665–1714), such spectacles continued to flourish.

THE BULL-AND-TERRIER

In the early 1800s, some Bulldog breeders tried something new, hoping to breed faster, fiercer fighters. They bred the most formidable

WHERE DID DOGS COME FROM?

It can be argued that dogs were right there at man's side from the beginning of time. As soon as human beings began to document their existence, the dog was among their drawings and inscriptions. Dogs were not just friends, they served a purpose: There were dogs to hunt birds, pull sleds, herd sheep, burrow after rats—even sit in laps! What your dog was originally bred to do influences the way he behaves. The American Kennel Club recognizes over 140 breeds, and there are hundreds more distinct breeds around the world. To make sense of the breeds, they are grouped according to their size or function. The AKC has seven groups:

1. Sporting
2. Working
3. Herding
4. Hounds
5. Terriers
6. Toys
7. Non Sporting

Can you name a breed from each group? Here's some help: (1) Golden Retriever, (2) Doberman Pinscher, (3) Collie, (4) Beagle, (5) Scottish Terrier, (6) Maltese and (7) Dalmatian. All modern domestic dogs (*Canis familiaris*) are related, however different they look, and are all descended from *Canis lupus*, the gray wolf.

baiting and fighting Bulldogs with the toughest, quickest and bravest terriers. This cross was believed to enhance the fighting ability of the Bulldog by reducing his size while maintaining his strength and increasing his speed and agility. Although some historians say the smooth-coated Black-and-Tan and the White English Terrier (now extinct) were most frequently crossed with Bulldogs, others say the terriers were chosen only on the basis of gameness and working ability, and that a variety of terrier-like dogs were used. The result of these crosses was called the Bull-and-Terrier or the Half-and-Half. As time passed and Bull-and-Terriers were selectively bred, they became recognizable as an emerging breed.

An early Bull-and-Terrier named Trusty was so famous in England that an article and picture of him appeared in an 1806 edition of *The Sporting Magazine*. The picture is the first one known of a Bull-and-Terrier cross. Trusty was "as renowned for his battles as Bonaparte," according to the article, and "fought 104 battles and was never beat." Raised by a prizefighter and later owned by a succession of boxers, Trusty was eventually purchased by Lord Camelford and came to be known as Lord Camelford's dog. Later, his lordship changed the dog's name to Belcher and presented him to fighting Jim Belcher, boxing champion of England. His lordship explained that "the only unconquered man was the only fit master for the only unconquered dog."

ARRIVAL IN AMERICA

Blood sports were popular in America, too, and the first Bulldogs and Bull-and-Terriers imported to the New World were brought over for that purpose. While bearbaiting was banned in New England as early as the 1600s, public spectacles such as bullbaiting, rat-killing competitions for dogs, dogfighting and cockfighting were extremely popular in New York City during the late seventeenth and early eighteenth centuries. Nearly all of America's early fighting dogs were British or Irish imports bred for generations to do battle, and many of the Americans who imported them continued breeding them for the same purpose.

Pit Bulls are descended from dogs that were bred to be the toughest, bravest fighters.

59

Dogfighting was so accepted in America that in 1881, when a fight was held in Louisville between the famed English imports, Lloyd's Pilot, owned by "Cockney Charlie" Lloyd, and Crib, owned by Louis Kreiger, the Ohio and Mississippi Railroad advertised special excursion fares to the big battle. Upon arrival in Louisville, bettors and spectators were taken to a fine hotel where they were warmly welcomed by the president of the Louisville board of aldermen, the police chief and other local officials. The referee for the fight was William Harding, sports editor of *The Police Gazette,* and owner-publisher Richard K. Fox served as stakeholder. Pilot and Crib

characters. Pit Bulls even graced the covers of *Life* on February 4, 1915, and again on March 24, 1917. The first picture, captioned "The Morning After," showed a bandaged and scarred Pit Bull; the later one, captioned "After Six," displayed a gentlemanly Pit Bull in a bow tie and top hat. Both were drawn by Will Rannells.

During World War I, the breed proved deserving of its country's esteem. A Pit Bull named Stubby was the war's most outstanding canine soldier. He earned the rank of sergeant, was mentioned in official dispatches and earned two medals, one for warning of a gas attack and the other for holding a German spy at Chemin des Dames until American troops arrived.

Following the war, the Pit Bull's popularity continued to grow. Depending on what it was used for and where it lived, the breed was still known by many different names, such as Bulldog, American Bull Terrier, Brindle Bull Dog, Yankee Terrier, Pit Dog, and, of course, American Pit Bull Terrier.

The first Pit Bull movie star was whelped on September 6, 1929. Pete, a brindle and white bred by

A. A. Keller, achieved fame on stage and screen as the dog actor in the *Little Rascals* and the *Our Gang* comedy series. Owned and trained by Harry Lucenay, Pete's UKC registered name was Lucenay's Peter.

During the mid 1970s, both Pit Bull registries, the UKC and the ADBA, began sanctioning shows for the breed. Since then, the number of Pit Bulls entered in shows has grown steadily.

THE PIT BULL TODAY

The real Pit Bull, the one registered with the UKC or the ADBA, is the same affectionate, reliable, hard-working, people-loving dog it ever was. A multitalented companion, the well-trained Pit Bull is suited for a variety of exciting activities. He excels at obedience, agility and weight-pulling competitions, events which showcase intelligence, train-ability and strength. In addition, the Pit Bull's pleasant nature makes him an ideal candidate for therapy work with people.

Today, because dog shows emphasize balanced structure and fluid movement, and obedience competition emphasizes trainability,

Today, Pit Bulls are bred to be affectionate family companions.

63

the Pit Bull is sometimes an even more attractive companion then he used to be. In addition, the breed still functions as a farm dog in rural America. The Pit Bull began his ranch work on the homesteads of frontier America and is still depended upon for varmint control, rounding up stock and sometimes even stopping and holding an angry steer.

The Pit Bull has always been a dog with a strong desire to please his owner. When that owner wanted him to fight, no matter how overmatched the dog was, the Pit Bull fought gamely. And today, when an enlightened owner raises him to be a happy, dependable family companion, that is exactly what he becomes. No dog does it better.

On Good Behavior

Dr. Ian Dunbar, Ph.D., MRCVS

T raining is the jewel in the crown—the most important aspect of doggy husbandry. There is no more important variable influencing dog behavior and temperament than the dog's education: A well-trained, well-behaved and good-natured puppydog is always a joy to live with, but an untrained and uncivilized dog can be a perpetual nightmare. Moreover, deny the dog an education and she will not have the opportunity to fulfill her own canine potential; neither will she have the ability to communicate effectively with her human companions.

Luckily, modern psychological training methods are easy, efficient, effective and, above all, considerably dog-friendly and user-friendly. Doggy education is as simple as it is enjoyable. But before you can have a good time play-training with your new dog, you have to learn what to do and how to do it. There is no bigger variable influencing the success of dog training than the owner's

Training your puppy is an opportunity to help her reach her own canine potential.

experience and expertise. Before you embark on the dog's education, you must first educate yourself.

BASIC TRAINING FOR OWNERS

Ideally, basic owner training should begin well before you select your dog. Find out all you can about your chosen breed first, then master rudimentary training and handling skills. If you already have your puppydog, owner training is a dire emergency—the clock is ticking! Especially for puppies, the first few weeks at home are the most important and influential days in the dog's life. Indeed, the cause of most adolescent and adult problems may be traced back to the initial days the pup explores her new home. This is the time to establish the

status quo—to teach the puppydog how you would like her to behave and so prevent otherwise quite predictable problems.

In addition to consulting breeders and breed books such as this one (which understandably have a positive breed bias), seek out as many pet owners with your breed as you can find. Good points are obvious. What you want to find out are the breed-specific problems, so you can nip them in the bud. In particular, you should talk to owners with adolescent dogs and make a list of all anticipated problems. Most important, test drive at least half a dozen adolescent and adult dogs of your breed yourself. An 8-week-old puppy is deceptively easy to handle, but she will acquire adult size, speed and strength in just four months, so you should learn now what to prepare for.

Puppy and pet dog training classes offer a convenient venue to locate pet owners and observe dogs in action. For a list of suitable trainers in your area, contact the Association of Pet Dog Trainers (see chapter 9). You may also begin your basic owner training by observing other owners in class. Watch as many classes and test drive as many dogs as possible. Select an upbeat, dog-friendly, people-friendly, fun-and-games, puppydog pet training class to learn the ropes. Also, watch training videos and read training books. You must find out what to do and how to do it *before* you have to do it.

PRINCIPLES OF TRAINING

Most people think training comprises teaching the dog to do things such as sit, speak and roll over, but even a 4-week-old pup knows how to do these things already. Instead, the first step in training involves teaching the dog human words for each dog behavior and activity and for each aspect of the dog's environment. That way you, the owner, can

The first few weeks at home are the time to teach your puppy how you would like her to behave.

more easily participate in the dog's domestic education by directing her to perform specific actions appropriately, that is, at the right time, in the right place and so on. Training opens communication channels, enabling an educated dog to at least understand her owner's requests.

In addition to teaching a dog what we want her to do, it is also necessary to teach her why she should do what we ask. Indeed, 95 percent of training revolves around motivating the dog to want to do what we want. Dogs often understand what their owners want; they just don't see the point of doing it—especially when the owner's repetitively boring and seemingly senseless instructions are totally at odds with much more pressing and exciting doggy distractions. It is not so much the dog that is being stubborn or dominant; rather, it is the owner who has failed to acknowledge the dog's needs and feelings and to approach training from the dog's point of view.

The Meaning of Instructions

The secret to successful training is learning how to use training lures to

The first step in training is teaching your dog human words that correspond with her behavior and activities.

67

predict or prompt specific behaviors—to coax the dog to do what you want when you want. Any highly valued object (such as a treat or toy) may be used as a lure, which the dog will follow with her eyes and nose. Moving the lure in specific ways entices the dog to move her nose, head and entire body in specific ways. In fact, by learning the art of manipulating various lures, it is possible to teach the dog to assume virtually any body position and perform any action. Once you have control over the expression of the dog's behaviors and can elicit any body position or behavior at will, you can easily teach the dog to perform on request.

OWNING A PARTY ANIMAL

It's a fact: The more of the world your puppy is exposed to, the more comfortable she'll be in it. Once your puppy's had her shots, start taking her everywhere with you. Encourage friendly interaction with strangers, expose her to different environments (towns, fields, beaches) and most important, enroll her in a puppy class where she'll get to play with other puppies. These simple, fun, shared activities will develop your pup into a confident socialite; reliable around other people and dogs.

Tell your dog what you want her to do, use a lure to entice her to respond correctly, then profusely praise and maybe reward her once she performs the desired action. For example, verbally request "Fido, sit!" while you move a squeaky toy upwards and backwards over the dog's muzzle (lure-movement and hand signal), smile knowingly as she looks up (to follow the lure) and sits down (as a result of canine anatomical engineering), then praise her to distraction ("Gooood Fido!"). Squeak the toy, offer a training treat and give your dog and yourself a pat on the back.

Being able to elicit desired responses over and over enables the owner to reward the dog over and over. Consequently, the dog begins to think training is fun. For example, the more the dog is rewarded for sitting, the more she enjoys sitting. Eventually the dog comes to realize that, whereas most sitting is appreciated, sitting immediately upon request usually prompts especially enthusiastic praise and a slew of high-level rewards. The dog begins to sit on cue much of the time, showing that she is starting to grasp the meaning of the owner's verbal request and hand signal.

Why Comply?

Most dogs enjoy initial lure-reward training and are only too happy to comply with their owners' wishes. Unfortunately, repetitive drilling without appreciative feedback tends to diminish the dog's enthusiasm until she eventually fails to see the point of complying anymore. Moreover, as the dog approaches adolescence she becomes more easily distracted as she develops other interests. Lengthy sessions with repetitive exercises tend to bore and demotivate both parties. If it's not fun, the owner doesn't do it and neither does the dog.

Integrate training into your dog's life: The greater number of training sessions each day and the shorter they are, the more willingly compliant your dog will become. Make sure to have a short (just a few seconds) training interlude before every enjoyable canine activity. For example, ask your dog to sit to greet people, to sit before you throw her Frisbee and to sit for her supper. Really, sitting is no different from a canine "Please." Also, include numerous short training interludes during every enjoyable canine pastime, for example, when playing with the dog or when she is running in the park. In this fashion, doggy distractions may be effectively converted into rewards for training. Just as all games have rules, fun becomes training . . . and training becomes fun.

Eventually, rewards actually become unnecessary to continue motivating your dog. If trained with consideration and kindness, performing the desired behaviors will become self-rewarding and, in a sense, your dog will motivate herself. Just as it is not necessary to reward a human companion during an enjoyable walk in the park, or following a game of tennis, it is hardly necessary to reward our best friend—the dog—for walking by our side or while playing fetch. Human company during enjoyable activities is reward enough for most dogs.

Even though your dog has become self-motivating, it's still good to praise and pet her a lot and offer rewards once in a while, especially for a job well done. And if for no other reason, praising and rewarding others is good for the human heart.

Punishment

Without a doubt, lure-reward training is by far the best way to teach: Entice your dog to do what you want and then reward her for doing so. Unfortunately, a human shortcoming is to take the good for granted and to moan and groan at the bad. Specifically, the dog's many good behaviors are ignored while the owner focuses on punishing the dog for making mistakes. In extreme cases, instruction is limited to punishing mistakes made by a trainee dog, child, employee or husband, even though it has been proven punishment training is notoriously

69

inefficient and ineffective and is decidedly unfriendly and combative. It teaches the dog that training is a drag, almost as quickly as it teaches the dog to dislike her trainer. Why treat our best friends like our worst enemies?

Punishment training is also much more laborious and time consuming. Whereas it takes only a finite amount of time to teach a dog what to chew, for example, it takes much, much longer to punish the dog for each and every mistake. Remember, there is only one right way! So why not teach that right way from the outset?!

To make matters worse, punishment training causes severe lapses in the dog's reliability. Since it is obviously impossible to punish the dog each and every time she misbehaves, the dog quickly learns to distinguish between those times when she must comply (so as to avoid impending punishment) and those times when she need not comply, because punishment is impossible. Such times include when the dog is off leash and 6 feet away, when the owner is otherwise engaged (talking to a friend, watching television, taking a shower, tending to the baby or chatting on the telephone) or when the dog is left at home alone.

Instances of misbehavior will be numerous when the owner is away, because even when the dog complied in the owner's looming presence, she did so unwillingly. The dog was forced to act against her will, rather than molding her will to want to please. Hence, when the owner is absent, not only does the dog know she need not comply, she simply does not want to. Again, the trainee is not a stubborn vindictive beast, but rather the trainer has failed to teach. Punishment training invariably creates unpredictable Jekyll and Hyde behavior.

TRAINER'S TOOLS

Many training books extol the virtues of a vast array of training paraphernalia and electronic and metallic gizmos, most of which are designed for canine restraint, correction and punishment, rather than for actual facilitation of doggy education. In reality, most effective training tools are not found in stores; they come from within ourselves. In addition to a willing dog, all you really need is a functional human brain, gentle hands, a loving heart and a good attitude.

In terms of equipment, all dogs do require a quality buckle collar to sport dog tags and to attach the leash (for safety and to comply with local leash laws). Hollow chew toys (like Kongs or sterilized longbones) and a dog bed or collapsible crate are musts for housetraining. Three additional tools are required:

1. specific lures (training treats and toys) to predict and prompt specific desired behaviors;

2. rewards (praise, affection, training treats and toys) to reinforce for the dog what a lot of fun it all is; and

3. knowledge—how to convert the dog's favorite activities and games (potential distractions to training) into "life-rewards," which may be employed to facilitate training.

The most powerful of these is knowledge. Education is the key! Watch training classes, participate in training classes, watch videos, read books, enjoy play-training with your dog and then your dog will say "Please," and your dog will say "Thank you!"

HOUSETRAINING

If dogs were left to their own devices, certainly they would chew, dig and bark for entertainment and then no doubt highlight a few areas of their living space with sprinkles of urine, in much the same way we decorate by hanging pictures. Consequently, when we ask a dog to live with us, we must teach her *where* she may dig, *where* she may perform her toilet duties, *what* she may chew and *when* she may bark. After all, when left at home alone for many hours, we cannot expect the dog to amuse herself by completing crosswords or watching TV!

Also, it would be decidedly unfair to keep the house rules a secret from the dog, and then get angry and punish the poor critter for inevitably transgressing rules she did not even know existed. Remember: Without adequate education and guidance, the dog will be forced to establish her own rules—doggy rules—and most probably will be at odds with the owner's view of domestic living.

Because most problems develop during the first few days the dog is at home, prospective dog owners must be certain they are quite clear

HOUSETRAINING 1-2-3

1. Prevent Mistakes. When you can't supervise your puppy, confine her in a single room or in her crate (but don't leave her for too long!). Puppy-proof the area by laying down newspapers so that if she does make a mistake, it won't matter.

2. Teach Where. Take your puppy to the spot you want her to use every hour.

3. When she goes, praise her profusely and give her three favorite treats.

about the principles of housetraining *before* they get a dog. Early misbehaviors quickly become established as the *status quo*—becoming firmly entrenched as hard-to-break bad habits, which set the precedent for years to come. Make sure to teach your dog good habits right from the start. Good habits are just as hard to break as bad ones!

Ideally, when a new dog comes home, try to arrange for someone to be present as much as possible during the first few days (for adult dogs) or weeks for puppies. With only a little forethought, it is surprisingly easy to find a puppy sitter, such as a retired person, who would be willing to eat from your refrigerator and watch your television while

keeping an eye on the newcomer to encourage the dog to play with chew toys and to ensure she goes outside on a regular basis.

Potty Training

Follow these steps to teach the dog where she should relieve herself:

1. never let her make a single mistake;

2. let her know where you want her to go; and

3. handsomely reward her for doing so: "GOOOOOOOD DOG!!!" liver treat, liver treat, liver treat!

Preventing Mistakes

A single mistake is a training disaster, since it heralds many more in future weeks. And each time the dog soils the house, this further reinforces the dog's unfortunate preference for an indoor, carpeted toilet. Do not let an unhousetrained dog have full run of the house.

When you are away from home, or cannot pay full attention, confine the dog to an area where elimination is appropriate, such as an outdoor run or, better still, a small, comfortable indoor kennel with access to an outdoor run. When confined in this manner, most dogs will naturally housetrain themselves.

If that's not possible, confine the dog to an area, such as a utility room, kitchen, basement or garage, where elimination may not be desired in the long run but as an interim measure it is certainly preferable to doing it all around the house. Use newspaper to cover the floor of the dog's day room. The newspaper may be used to soak up the urine and to wrap up and dispose of the feces. Once your dog develops a preferred spot for eliminating, it is only necessary to cover that part of the floor with newspaper. The smaller papered area may then be moved (only a little each day) towards the door to the outside. Thus the dog will develop the tendency to go to the door when she needs to relieve herself.

Never confine an unhousetrained dog to a crate for long periods. Doing so would force the dog to soil the crate and ruin its usefulness as an aid for housetraining (see the following discussion).

Teaching Where

In order to teach your dog where you would like her to do her

business, you have to be there to direct the proceedings—an obvious, yet often neglected, fact of life. In order to be there to teach the dog where to go, you need to know *when* she needs to go. Indeed, the success of housetraining depends on the owner's ability to predict these times. Certainly, a regular feeding schedule will facilitate prediction somewhat, but there is nothing like "loading the deck" and influencing the timing of the outcome yourself!

Whenever you are at home, make sure the dog is under constant supervision and/or confined to a small area. If already well trained, simply instruct the dog to lie down in her bed or basket. Alternatively, confine the dog to a crate (doggy den) or tie-down (a short, 18-inch lead that can be clipped to an eye hook in the baseboard near her bed). Short-term close confinement strongly inhibits urination and defecation, since the dog does not want to soil her sleeping area. Thus, when you release the puppydog each hour, she will definitely need to urinate immediately and defecate every third or fourth hour. Keep the dog confined to her doggy den and take her to her intended toilet area each hour, every hour and on the hour.

73

When taking your dog outside, instruct her to sit quietly before opening the door—she will soon learn to sit by the door when she needs to go out!

Teaching Why

Being able to predict when the dog needs to go enables the owner to be on the spot to praise and reward the dog. Each hour, hurry the dog to the intended toilet area in the yard, issue the appropriate instruction ("Go pee!" or "Go poop!"), then give the dog three to four minutes to produce. Praise and offer a couple of training treats when successful. The treats are important because many people fail to praise their dogs with feeling . . . and housetraining is hardly the time for understatement. So either loosen up and enthusiastically praise that dog: "Wuzzzzer-wuzzer-wuzzer, hoooser good wuffer den? Hoooo went pee for Daddy?" Or say "Good dog!" as best you can and offer the treats for effect.

Following elimination is an ideal time for a spot of play-training in the yard or house. Also, an empty dog may be allowed greater freedom around the house for the next half hour or so, just as long as you keep

an eye out to make sure she does not get into other kinds of mischief. If you are preoccupied and cannot pay full attention, confine the dog to her doggy den once more to enjoy a peaceful snooze or to play with her many chew toys.

If your dog does not eliminate within the allotted time outside—no biggie! Back to her doggy den, and then try again after another hour.

As I own large dogs, I always feel more relaxed walking an empty dog, knowing that I will not need to finish our stroll weighted down with bags of feces!

Beware of falling into the trap of walking the dog to get her to eliminate. The good ol' dog walk is such an enormous highlight in the dog's life that it represents the single biggest potential reward in domestic dogdom. However, when in a hurry, or during inclement weather, many owners abruptly terminate the walk the moment the dog has done her business. This, in effect, severely punishes the dog for doing the right thing, in the right place at the right time. Consequently, many dogs become strongly inhibited from eliminating outdoors because they know it will signal an abrupt end to an otherwise thoroughly enjoyable walk.

Instead, instruct the dog to relieve herself in the yard prior to going for a walk. If you follow the above instructions, most dogs soon learn to eliminate on cue. As soon as the dog eliminates, praise (and offer a treat or two)—"Good dog! Let's go walkies!" Use the walk as a reward for eliminating in the yard. If the dog does not go, put her back in her doggy den and think about a walk later on. You will find with a "No feces—no walk" policy, your dog will become one of the fastest defecators in the business.

If you do not have a backyard, instruct the dog to eliminate right outside your front door prior to the walk. Not only will this facilitate clean up and disposal of the feces in your own trash can but, also, the walk may again be used as a colossal reward.

CHEWING AND BARKING

Short-term close confinement also teaches the dog that occasional quiet moments are a reality of domestic living. Your puppydog is extremely impressionable during her first few weeks at home. Regular confinement at this time soon exerts a calming influence over the dog's personality. Remember, once the dog is housetrained and calmer, there will be a whole lifetime ahead for the dog to enjoy full run of the house and garden. On the other hand, by letting the newcomer have unrestricted access to the entire household and allowing her to run willy-nilly, she will most certainly develop a bunch of behavior problems in short order, no doubt necessitating confinement later in life. It would not be fair to remedially restrain and confine a dog you have trained, through neglect, to run free.

When confining the dog, make sure she always has an impressive array of suitable chew toys. Kongs and sterilized longbones (both readily available from pet stores) make the best chew toys, since they are hollow and may be stuffed with treats to heighten the dog's interest. For example, by stuffing the little hole at the top of a Kong with a small piece of freeze-dried liver, the dog will not want to leave it alone.

Remember, treats do not have to be junk food and they certainly should not represent extra calories. Rather, treats should be part of each dog's regular daily diet.

FINDING A TRAINER

Have fun with your dog, take a training class! But don't just sign on any dotted line, find a trainer whose approach and style you like and whose students (and their dogs) are really learning. Ask to visit a class to observe a trainer in action. For the names of trainers near you, ask your veterinarian, your pet supply store, your dog-owning neighbors or call (800) PET-DOGS (the Association of Pet Dog Trainers).

COME AND SIT

Most puppies will happily approach virtually anyone, whether called or not; that is, until they collide with adolescence and develop other more important doggy interests, such as sniffing a multiplicity of exquisite odors on the grass. Your mission, Mr./Ms. Owner, is to teach and reward the pup for coming reliably, willingly and happily when called— and you have just three months to get it done. Unless adequately reinforced, your puppy's tendency to approach people will self-destruct by adolescence.

Call your dog ("Fido, come!"), open your arms (and maybe squat down) as a welcoming signal, waggle a treat or toy as a lure and reward

the puppydog when she comes running. Do not wait to praise the dog until she reaches you—she may come 95 percent of the way and then run off after some distraction. Instead, praise the dog's first step towards you and continue praising enthusiastically for every step she takes in your direction.

When the rapidly approaching puppy dog is three lengths away from impact, instruct her to sit ("Fido, sit!") and hold the lure in front of you in an outstretched hand to prevent her from hitting you mid-chest and knocking you flat on your back! As Fido decelerates to nose the lure, move the treat upwards and backwards just over her muzzle with an upwards motion of your extended arm (palm-upwards). As the dog looks up to follow the lure, she will sit down (if she jumps up, you are holding the lure too high). Praise the dog for sitting. Move backwards and call her again. Repeat this many times over, always praising when Fido comes and sits; on occasion, reward her.

For the first couple of trials, use a training treat both as a lure to entice the dog to come and sit and as a reward for doing so. Thereafter, try to use different items as lures and rewards. For example, lure the dog with a Kong or Frisbee but reward her with a food treat. Or lure the dog with a food treat but pat her and throw a tennis ball as a reward. After just a few repetitions, dispense with the lures and rewards; the dog will begin to respond willingly to your verbal requests and hand signals just for the prospect of praise from your heart and affection from your hands.

Instruct every family member, friend and visitor how to get the dog to come and sit. Invite people over for a series of pooch parties; do not keep the pup a secret—let other people enjoy this puppy, and let the pup enjoy other people. Puppydog parties are not only fun, they easily attract a lot of people to help you train your dog. Unless you teach your dog how to meet people, that is, to sit for greetings, no doubt the dog will resort to jumping up. Then you and the visitors will get annoyed, and the dog will be punished. This is not fair. Send out those invitations for puppy parties and teach your dog to be mannerly and socially acceptable.

Even though your dog quickly masters obedient recalls in the house, her reliability may falter when playing in the backyard or local park. Ironically, it is the owner who has unintentionally trained the dog not to respond in these instances. By allowing the dog to play and run around and otherwise have a good time, but then to call the dog to put her on leash to take her home, the dog quickly learns playing is fun but training is a drag.

To teach come, call your dog, open your arms as a welcoming signal, wave a toy or a treat and praise for every step in your direction.

Thus, playing in the park becomes a severe distraction, which works against training. Bad news!

Instead, whether playing with the dog off leash or on leash, request her to come at frequent intervals—say, every minute or so. On most occasions, praise and pet the dog for a few seconds while she is sitting, then tell her to go play again. For especially fast recalls, offer a couple of training treats and take the time to praise and pet the dog enthusiastically before releasing her. The dog will learn that coming when called is not necessarily the end of the play session, and neither is it the end of the world; rather, it signals an enjoyable, quality time-out with the owner before resuming play once more. In fact, playing in the park now becomes a very effective life-reward, which works to facilitate training by reinforcing each obedient and timely recall. Good news!

SIT, DOWN, STAND AND ROLLOVER

Teaching the dog a variety of body positions is easy for owner and dog, impressive for spectators and extremely useful for all. Using lure-reward techniques, it is possible to train several positions at once to verbal commands or hand signals (which impress the socks off onlookers).

Sit and down—the two control commands—prevent or resolve nearly a hundred behavior problems. For example, if the dog happily and obediently sits or lies down when requested, she cannot jump on visitors, dash out the front door, run around and chase her tail, pester other dogs, harass cats or annoy family, friends or strangers. Additionally, "Sit" or "Down" are the best emergency commands for off-leash control.

It is easier to teach and maintain a reliable sit than maintain a reliable recall. Sit is the purest and simplest of commands—either the dog is sitting or she is not. If there is any change of circumstances or potential danger in the park, for example, simply instruct the dog to sit. If she sits, you have a number of options: Allow the dog to resume playing when she is safe, walk up and put the dog on leash or call the dog. The dog will be much more likely to come when called if she has already acknowledged her compliance by sitting. If the dog does not sit in the park—train her to!

Stand and rollover-stay are the two positions for examining the dog. Your veterinarian will love you to distraction if you take a little time to teach the dog to stand still and roll over and play possum. Also, your vet bills will be smaller because it will take the veterinarian less time to examine your dog. The rollover-stay is an especially useful command and is really just a variation of the down-stay: Whereas the dog lies prone in the traditional down, she lies supine in the rollover-stay.

As with teaching come and sit, the training techniques to teach the dog to assume all other body positions on cue are user-friendly and dog-friendly. Simply give the appropriate request, lure the dog into the desired body position using a training treat or toy and then praise (and maybe reward) the dog as soon as she complies. Try not to touch the dog to get her to respond. If you teach the dog by guiding her into position, the dog will quickly learn that rump-pressure means sit, for example, but as yet you still have no control over your dog if she is just 6 feet away. It will still be necessary to teach the dog to sit on request. So do not make training a time-consuming two-step process;

instead, teach the dog to sit to a verbal request or hand signal from the outset. Once the dog sits willingly when requested, by all means use your hands to pet the dog when she does so.

To teach down when the dog is already sitting, say "Fido, down!", hold the lure in one hand (palm down) and lower that hand to the floor between the dog's forepaws. As the dog lowers her head to follow the lure, slowly move the lure away from the dog just a fraction (in front of her paws). The dog will lie down as she stretches her nose forward to follow the lure. Praise the dog when she does so. If the dog stands up, you pulled the lure away too far and too quickly.

When teaching the dog to lie down from the standing position, say "Down" and lower the lure to the floor as before. Once the dog has lowered her forequarters and assumed a play bow, gently and slowly move the lure towards the dog between her forelegs. Praise the dog as soon as her rear end plops down.

After just a couple of trials it will be possible to alternate sits and downs and have the dog energetically perform doggy push-ups. Praise the dog a lot, and after half a dozen or so push-ups reward the dog with a training treat or toy. You will notice the more energetically you move your arm—upwards (palm up) to get the dog to sit, and downwards (palm down) to get the dog to lie down—the more energetically the dog responds to your requests. Now try training the dog in silence and you will notice she has also learned to respond to hand signals. Yeah! Not too shabby for the first session.

To teach stand from the sitting position, say "Fido, stand," slowly move the lure half a dog-length away from the dog's nose, keeping it at nose level, and praise the dog as she stands to follow the lure. As soon as the dog stands, lower the lure to just beneath the dog's chin to entice her to look down; otherwise she will stand and then sit immediately. To prompt the dog to stand from the down position, move the lure half a dog-length upwards and away from the dog, holding the lure at standing nose height from the floor.

Teaching rollover is best started from the down position, with the dog lying on one side, or at least with both hind legs stretched out on

the same side. Say "Fido, bang!" and move the lure backwards and alongside the dog's muzzle to her elbow (on the side of her outstretched hind legs). Once the dog looks to the side and backwards, very slowly move the lure upwards to the dog's shoulder and backbone. Tickling the dog in the goolies (groin area) often invokes a reflex-raising of the hind leg as an appeasement gesture, which facilitates the tendency to roll over. If you move the lure too quickly and the dog jumps into the standing position, have patience and start again. As soon as the dog rolls onto her back, keep the lure stationary and mesmerize the dog with a relaxing tummy rub.

To teach rollover-stay when the dog is standing or moving, say "Fido, bang!" and give the appropriate hand signal (with index finger pointed and thumb cocked in true Sam Spade fashion), then in one fluid movement lure her to first lie down and then rollover-stay as above.

Teaching the dog to stay in each of the above four positions becomes a piece of cake after first teaching the dog not to worry at the toy or treat training lure. This is best accomplished by hand feeding dinner kibble. Hold a piece of kibble firmly in your hand and softly instruct "Off!" Ignore any licking and slobbering for however long the dog worries at the treat, but say "Take it!" and offer the kibble the instant the dog breaks contact with her muzzle. Repeat this a few times, and then up the ante and insist the dog remove her muzzle for one whole second before offering the kibble. Then progressively refine your criteria and have the dog not touch your hand (or treat) for longer and longer periods on each trial, such as for two seconds, four seconds, then six, ten, fifteen, twenty, thirty seconds and so on.

The dog soon learns: (1) worrying at the treat never gets results, whereas (2) noncontact is often rewarded after a variable time lapse.

Teaching "Off!" has many useful applications in its own right. Additionally, instructing the dog not to touch a training lure often produces spontaneous and magical stays. Request the dog to stand-stay, for example, and not to touch the lure. At first set your sights on a short two-second stay before rewarding the dog. (Remember, every long journey begins with a single step.) However, on subsequent trials, gradually and progressively increase the length of stay required to receive a reward. In no time at all your dog will stand calmly for a minute or so.

RELEVANCY TRAINING

Once you have taught the dog what you expect her to do when requested to come, sit, lie down, stand, rollover and stay, the time is right to teach the dog why she should comply with your wishes. The secret is to have many (many) extremely short training interludes (two to five seconds each) at numerous (numerous) times during the course of the dog's day. Especially work with the dog immediately before the dog's good times and during the dog's good times. For example, ask your dog to sit and/or lie down each time before opening doors, serving meals, offering treats and tummy rubs; ask the dog to perform a few controlled doggy pushups before letting her off leash or throwing a tennis ball; and perhaps request the dog to sit-down-sit-stand-down-stand-rollover before inviting her to cuddle on the couch.

Similarly, request the dog to sit many times during play or on walks, and in no time at all the dog will be only too pleased to follow your instructions because she has learned that a compliant response heralds all sorts of goodies. Basically all you are trying to teach the dog is how to say please: "Please throw the tennis ball. Please may I snuggle on the couch."

Remember, it is important to keep training interludes short and to have many short sessions each and every day. The shortest (and most useful) session comprises asking the dog to sit and then go play during a play session. When trained this way, your dog will soon associate training with good times. In fact, the dog may be unable to distinguish between training and good times and, indeed, there should be no distinction. The warped concept that training involves forcing the dog to comply and/or dominating her will is totally at odds with the picture of a truly well-trained dog. In reality, enjoying a game of training with a dog is no different from enjoying a game of backgammon or tennis with a friend; and walking with a dog should be no different from strolling with a spouse, or with buddies on the golf course.

WALK BY YOUR SIDE

Many people attempt to teach a dog to heel by putting her on a leash and physically correcting the dog when she makes mistakes. There are a number of things seriously wrong with this approach, the first being that most people do not want precision heeling; rather, they simply want the dog to follow or walk by their side. Second, when physically restrained during "training," even though the dog may grudgingly mope by your side when "handcuffed" on leash, let's see what happens when she is off leash. History! The dog is in the next county because she never enjoyed walking with you on leash and you have no control over her off leash. So let's just teach the dog off leash from the outset to want to walk with us. Third, if the dog has not been trained to heel, it is a trifle hasty to think about punishing the poor dog for making mistakes and breaking heeling rules she didn't even know existed. This is simply not fair! Surely, if the dog had been adequately taught how to heel, she would seldom make mistakes and hence there would be no need to correct the dog. Remember, each mistake and each correction (punishment) advertise the trainer's inadequacy, not the dog's. The dog is not stubborn, she is not stupid and she is not bad. Even if she were, she would still require training, so let's train her properly.

Let's teach the dog to enjoy following us and to want to walk by our side off leash. Then it will be easier to teach high-precision off-leash heeling patterns if desired. Before going on outdoor walks, it is necessary to teach the dog not to pull. Then it becomes easy to teach on-leash walking and heeling because the dog already wants to walk with you, she is familiar with the desired walking and heeling positions and she knows not to pull.

FOLLOWING

Start by training your dog to follow you. Many puppies will follow if you simply walk away from them and maybe click your fingers or chuckle. Adult dogs may require additional enticement to stimulate them to follow, such as a training lure or, at the very least, a lively trainer. To teach the dog to follow: (1) keep walking and (2) walk away from the dog. If

Keep training sessions short, fun and frequent.

the dog attempts to lead or lag, change pace; slow down if the dog forges too far ahead, but speed up if she lags too far behind. Say "Steady!" or "Easy!" each time before you slow down and "Quickly!" or "Hustle!" each time before you speed up, and the dog will learn to change pace on cue. If the dog lags or leads too far, or if she wanders right or left, simply walk quickly in the opposite direction and maybe even run away from the dog and hide.

Practicing is a lot of fun; you can set up a course in your home, yard or park to do this. Indoors, entice the dog to follow upstairs, into a bedroom, into the bathroom, downstairs, around the living room couch,

Because dogs love going for walks, use them as rewards for quick and easy training sessions.

BY YOUR SIDE

It is smart to train the dog to walk close on one side or the other—either side will do, your choice. When walking, jogging or cycling, it is generally bad news to have the dog suddenly cut in front of you. In fact, I train my dogs to walk "By my side" and "Other side"—both very useful instructions. It is possible to position the dog fairly accurately by looking to the appropriate side and clicking your fingers or slapping your thigh on that side. A precise positioning may be attained by holding a training lure, such as a chew toy, tennis ball, or food treat. Stop and stand still several times throughout the walk, just as you would when window shopping or meeting a friend. Use the lure to make sure the dog slows down and stays close whenever you stop.

When teaching the dog to heel, we generally want her to sit in heel position when we stop. Teach heel position at the standstill and the dog will learn that the default heel position is sitting by your side (left or right—your choice, unless you wish to compete in obedience trials, in which case the dog must heel on the left).

zigzagging between dining room chairs and into the kitchen for dinner. Outdoors, get the dog to follow around park benches, trees, shrubs and along walkways and lines in the grass. (For safety outdoors, it is advisable to attach a long line on the dog, but never exert corrective tension on the line.)

Remember, following has a lot to do with attitude—your attitude! Most probably your dog will not want to follow Mr. Grumpy Troll with the personality of wilted lettuce. Lighten up—walk with a jaunty step, whistle a happy tune, sing, skip and tell jokes to your dog and she will be right there by your side.

Several times a day, stand up and call your dog to come and sit in heel position—"Fido, heel!" For example, instruct the dog to come to heel each time there are commercials on TV, or each time you turn a page of a novel, and the dog will get it in a single evening.

Practice straight-line heeling and turns separately. With the dog sitting at heel, teach her to turn in place. After each quarter-turn, half-turn or full turn in place, lure the dog to sit at heel. Now it's time for short straight-line heeling sequences, no more than a few steps at a time. Always think of heeling in terms of sit-heel-sit sequences—start and end with the dog in position and do your best to keep her there when moving. Progressively increase the number of steps in each sequence. When the dog remains close for 20 yards of straight-line heeling, it is time to add a few turns and then sign up for a happy-heeling obedience class to get some advice from the experts.

No Pulling on Leash

You can start teaching your dog not to pull on leash anywhere—in front

Toys that Earn Their Keep

To entertain even the most distracted of dogs, while you're home or away, have a selection of the following toys on hand: hollow chew toys (like Kongs, sterilized hollow longbones and cubes or balls that can be stuffed with kibble). Smear peanut butter or honey on the inside of the hollow toy or bone and stuff the bone with kibble and your dog will think of nothing else but working the object to get at the food. Great to take your dog's mind off the fact that you've left the house.

of the television or outdoors—but regardless of location, you must not take a single step with tension in the leash. For a reason known only to dogs, even just a couple of paces of pulling on leash is intrinsically motivating and diabolically rewarding. Instead, attach the leash to the dog's collar, grasp the other end firmly with both hands held close to your chest, and stand still—do not budge an inch. Have somebody watch you with a stopwatch to time your progress, or else you will never believe this will work and so you will not even try the exercise, and your shoulder and the dog's neck will be traumatized for years to come.

With their abundant energy, Pit Bulls will find ways to exercise—this might not be the training you intend!

Stand still and wait for the dog to stop pulling, and to sit and/or lie down. All dogs stop pulling and sit eventually. Most take only a couple of minutes; the all-time record is 22¹/₂ minutes. Time how long it takes. Gently praise the dog when she stops pulling, and as soon as she sits, enthusiastically praise the dog and take just one step forwards, then immediately stand still. This single step usually demonstrates the ballistic reinforcing nature of pulling on leash; most dogs explode to the end of the leash, so be prepared for the strain. Stand firm and wait for the dog to sit again. Repeat this half a dozen times and you will probably notice a progressive reduction in the force of the dog's one-step explosions and a radical reduction in the time it takes for the dog to sit each time.

As the dog learns "Sit we go" and "Pull we stop," she will begin to walk forward calmly with each single step and automatically sit when you stop. Now try two steps before you stop. Wooooooo! Scary! When the dog has mastered two steps at a time, try for three. After each success, progressively increase the number of steps in the sequence: try four steps and then six, eight, ten and twenty steps before stopping. Congratulations! You are now walking the dog on leash.

Whenever walking with the dog (off leash or on leash), make sure you stop periodically to practice a few position commands and stays before instructing the dog to "Walk on!"

Integrating training into a walk offers 200 separate opportunities to use the continuance of the walk as a reward to reinforce the dog's education.

Resources

BOOKS

About Pit Bulls

Fraser, Jacqueline. *The Ultimate American Pit Bull Terrier*. New York: Howell Book House, 1995.

Semencic, Carl. *Pit Bulls and Tenacious Guard Dogs*. Neptune, N.J.: TFH Publications, 1991.

Stratton, Richard F. *The World of the American Pit Bull Terrier*. Neptune, N.J.: TFH Publications, 1983.

About Health Care

American Kennel Club. *American Kennel Club Dog Care and Training*. New York: Howell Book House, 1991.

Carlson, Delbert, DVM, and James Giffen, MD. *Dog Owner's Home Veterinary Handbook*. New York: Howell Book House, 1992.

DeBitetto, James, DVM, and Sarah Hodgson. *You & Your Puppy*. New York: Howell Book House, 1995.

Lane, Marion. *The Humane Society of the United States Complete Guide to Dog Care*. New York: Little, Brown & Co., 1998.

McGinnis, Terri. *The Well Dog Book*. New York: Random House, 1991.

Schwartz, Stephanie, DVM. *First Aid for Dogs: An Owner's Guide to a Happy Healthy Pet*. New York: Howell Book House, 1998.

Volhard, Wendy and Kerry L. Brown. *The Holistic Guide for a Healthy Dog*. New York: Howell Book House, 1995.

About Training

Ammen, Amy. *Training in No Time*. New York: Howell Book House, 1995.

Benjamin, Carol Lea. *Mother Knows Best*. New York: Howell Book House, 1985.

Bohnenkamp, Gwen. *Manners for the Modern Dog*. San Francisco: Perfect Paws, 1990.

Dunbar, Ian, Ph.D., MRCVS. *Dr. Dunbar's Good Little Book.* James & Kenneth Publishers, 2140 Shattuck Ave. #2406, Berkeley, CA 94704. (510) 658-8588. Order from Publisher.

Evans, Job Michael. *People, Pooches and Problems.* New York: Howell Book House, 1991.

Palika, Liz. *All Dogs Need Some Training.* New York: Howell Book House, 1997.

Volhard, Jack and Melissa Bartlett. *What All Good Dogs Should Know: The Sensible Way to Train.* New York: Howell Book House, 1991.

About Activities

Hall, Lynn. *Dog Showing for Beginners.* New York: Howell Book House, 1994.

O'Neil, Jackie. *All About Agility.* New York: Howell Book House, 1998.

Simmons-Moake, Jane. *Agility Training, The Fun Sport for All Dogs.* New York: Howell Book House, 1991.

Vanacore, Connie. *Dog Showing: An Owner's Guide.* New York: Howell Book House, 1990.

Volhard, Jack and Wendy. *The Canine Good Citizen.* New York: Howell Book House, 1994.

MAGAZINES

THE AKC GAZETTE, The Official Journal for the Sport of Purebred Dogs
American Kennel Club
260 Madison Ave.
New York, NY 10016
www.akc.org

THE AMERICAN PIT BULL TERRIER GAZETTE
American Dog Breeder's Association
Box 1771
Salt Lake City, UT 84110

DOG FANCY
Fancy Publications
3 Burroughs
Irvine, CA 92618
(714) 855-8822
http://dogfancy.com

DOG & KENNEL
7-L Dundas Circle
Greensboro, NC 27407
(336) 292-4047
www.dogandkennel.com

DOG WORLD
Maclean Hunter Publishing Corp.
500 N. Dearborn, Ste. 1100
Chicago, IL 60610
(312) 396-0600
www.dogworldmag.com

PETLIFE: *Your Companion Animal Magazine*
Magnolia Media Group
1400 Two Tandy Center
Fort Worth, TX 76102
(800) 767-9377
www.petlifeweb.com

MORE INFORMATION ABOUT PIT BULLS

THE AMERICAN DOG
BREEDER'S ASSOCIATION, INC.
Box 1771
Salt Lake City, UT 84110

The club can send you information on all aspects of the breed, including the names and addresses of breed clubs in your area, as well as obedience clubs. Inquire about membership.

UNITED KENNEL CLUB
100 E. Kilgore Rd.
Kalamazoo, MI 49001-5598
(616) 343-9020
www.ukcdogs.com

AMERICAN RARE BREED
ASSOCIATION
9921 Frank Tippett Rd.
Cheltenham, MD 20623
(301) 868-5718 (voice or fax)
www.arba.org

CANADIAN KENNEL CLUB
89 Skyway Ave., Ste. 100
Etobicoke, Ontario
Canada M9W 6R4
(416) 675-5511
www.ckc.ca

ORTHOPEDIC FOUNDATION
FOR ANIMALS (OFA)
2300 E. Nifong Blvd.
Columbia, MO 65201-3856
(314) 442-0418
www.offa.org/

Trainers

Animal Behavior & Training Associates
(ABTA)
9018 Balboa Blvd., Ste. 591
Northridge, CA 91325
(800) 795-3294
www.Good-dawg.com

Association of Pet Dog Trainers
(APDT)
(800) PET-DOGS
www.apdt.com

National Association of Dog Obedience
Instructors (NADOI)
729 Grapevine Highway, Ste. 369
Hurst, TX 76054-2085
www.kimberly.uidaho.edu/nadoi

Associations

Delta Society
P.O. Box 1080
Renton, WA 98507-1080
(Promotes the human/animal bond through pet-assisted therapy and other programs)
www.petsforum.com/
DELTASOCIETY/dsi400.htm

Dog Writers Association of America
(DWAA)
Sally Cooper, Secretary
222 Woodchuck Lane
Harwinton, CT 06791
www.dwaa.org

National Association for Search and
Rescue (NASAR)
4500 Southgate Place, Ste. 100
Chantilly, VA 20157
(703) 222-6277
www.nasar.org

Therapy Dogs International
6 Hilltop Rd.
Mendham, NJ 07945

OTHER USEFUL RESOURCES— WEB SITES

General Information— Links to Additional Sites, On-Line Shopping

www.k9web.com – resources for the dog world

www.netpet.com – pet related products, software and services

www.apapets.com – The American Pet Association

www.dogandcatbooks.com – book catalog

www.dogbooks.com – on-line bookshop

www.animal.discovery.com/ – cable television channel on-line

Health

www.avma.org – American Veterinary Medical Association (AVMA)

www.aplb.org – Association for Pet Loss Bereavement (APLB)—contains an index of national hot lines for on-line and office counseling.

www.netfopets.com/AskTheExperts. html – veterinary questions answered on-line.

Breed Information

www.bestdogs.com/news/ – newsgroup

www.cheta.net/connect/canine/breeds/ – Canine Connections Breed Information Index